PRINTED IN ITALY BY ARNOLDO MONDADORI EDITORE OFFICINE GRAFICHE

The Past We Share

The

PROMETHEUS PRESS

New York 1960

© PETER QUENNELL AND ALAN HODGE

Past We Share

An illustrated history of the British and American peoples

Edited by PETER QUENNELL *and* ALAN HODGE

Contents

Colour Plates

Acknowledgments

The following illustrations are reproduced by gracious permission of HER MAJESTY THE QUEEN, 2, 105, 106, 108, 115, 118, 162, 169, 176, 227, 230, 259, 291, 293, 330, 371, 373, 396, 456, 462, 463. The publishers also wish to thank the following public and private owners and sources for kind permission to reproduce illustrations: SIR WILLIAM ACLAND, BT., 477; AEROFILMS LTD., 109; THOMAS AGNEW & SONS LTD., 324; ALBRIGHT ART GALLERY, Buffalo, New York, 432; LYMAN ALLYN MUSEUM, New London, Connecticut, 448; HOUSE OF DELEGATES, Annapolis, Maryland (and *Time-Life*), Pl. XIII; ASHMOLEAN MUSEUM, Oxford, 239, 250; ASSOCIATED PRESS, 567; BARRATT'S PHOTO AGENCY, 540; ÖFFENTLICHE KUNSTSAMMLUNG, Basle, 104; MESSRS BATSFORD, 480, 481, 485, 489, 490; HIS GRACE THE DUKE OF BEDFORD, 99, 133; BIBLIOTHÈQUE NATIONALE, Paris, 418; BOATMEN'S NATIONAL BANK OF ST LOUIS, Missouri, 419; BODLEIAN LIBRARY, Oxford, 37, 58–62, 74, 126; CITY OF BOSTON (*on loan to Museum of Fine Arts*, Boston, 334; MUSEUM OF FINE ARTS, Boston, 352, 354 (M. & M. Karolik Collection); EARL OF BRADFORD, 94; BRISTOL CITY ART GALLERY, 423; BRITISH MUSEUM, Pls. II, III (and *Time-Life*), VIII (and *American Heritage*), and 4, 12, 39, 40, 42–5, 54–7, 66, 71, 76, 80, 88 89, 96, 122, 136, 144, 147, 153, 157, 164, 179, 184, 205 9, 226, 234–7, 256, 261, 287, 296, 300, 305, 307, 311, 379, 392, 397, 408, 437, 438, 440, 486, 491, 520; BRITISH OFFICIAL PHOTOGRAPHS, 595; BROWN UNIVERSITY LIBRARY, Providence, Rhode Island, 442; HIS GRACE THE DUKE OF BUCCLEUGH, 165; MARQUESS OF BUTE, 377; W. A. CALL, Monmouth, 39; CAMERA PRESS, 599; HIS GRACE THE ARCHIBISHOP OF CANTERBURY AND THE CHURCH COMMISSIONERS, 64, 68, 114, 130; SIR JOHN CAREW-POLE, BT., 149; J. ALLAN CASH, 52, 74, 110, 253, 273, 301; MARQUESS OF CHOLMONDELEY, 295, 317; MARCHIONESS OF CHOLMONDELEY, 232, 401; CHRIST CHURCH, Oxford, 291; CHURCHILL COLLEGE, Cambridge, Trust Fund, 383; MUSEUM OF THE CITY OF NEW YORK, 214, 215, 426; LIBRARY OF CONGRESS, Washington, 517, 521; COPYRIGHT RESERVED, 187, 188; CRAFTSBURY PUBLIC LIBRARY, Vermont, 353; MARCHIONESS OF CREWE, 393; DULWICH COLLEGE, London, 156; SIR CLIVE EDWARDS, BT., 159; MESSRS ELLIOT & FRY, 542; ETON COLLEGE, Windsor, 13, 394; EXCLUSIVE NEWS AGENCY, 526, 534, 538, 541, 577; EARL FITZWILLIAM, 312; FOGG ART MUSEUM, Harvard, 337; HARRIETTE MERRIFIELD FORBES, 202; MRS J. C. FRAZER, Washington, 356; FRICK COLLECTION, New York, 363; EDGAR WILLIAM AND BERNICE CHRYSLER, GARBISCH, Washington, 351, 354, 430, 431, 436, 446, 447, 450; D. W. GARDNER, 75; GEORGE GOYDER, ESQ., 113; GUILDHALL MUSEUM, London, 182, 231, 386; MESSRS HEINEMANN, 544; HENRY E. HUNTINGTON LIBRARY, California (and *American Heritage*), Pl. IX; MARTIN HÜRLIMANN, Atlantis Verlag, Zürich, 24, 48, 53, 73, 85–7; IMPERIAL WAR MUSEUM, London, 6, 539, 559–61; INDEPENDENCE NATIONAL HISTORICAL PARK COLLECTION, Philadelphia, 359, 361; INDEPENDENT NEWS PHOTOS, 585; INDIA OFFICE LIBRARY (Commonwealth Relations Office), 469; INNER TEMPLE LIBRARY, London, 86; A. F. KERSTING, 34, 35, 83, 141, 142, 143, 177, 267, 275, 276, 318, 320, 375; KEYSTONE, 566, 584, 586, 587–9, 592, 594, 600; KÜNSTHISTORISCHES MUSEUM, Vienna, 95; LEEDS CITY ART GALLERY, 380; COLONEL J. L. LEICESTER-WARREN, 172; MARQUESS OF LINLITHGOW, 292; LONDON MUSEUM, 537; MESSRS LONGMANS, 279; MANSELL COLLECTION, London, 185, 212, 340, 416, 428, 444, 471–4, 487, 488, 498, 504, 509, 518, 527, 532; MESSRS MANTEAU, 222; HIS GRACE THE DUKE OF MARLBOROUGH, 269; MASSACHUSETTS HISTORICAL SOCIETY, 195, 200, 201; MAURITSHUIS, The Hague, 107; METROPOLITAN MUSEUM OF ART, New York, 252, 331, 336, 350, 355, 358, 368, 387, 422; A. F. MONDSCHEIN, 427, 434; ADMIRAL OF THE FLEET EARL MOUNTBATTEN, 178, 413; SIR JOHN MURRAY, 399; NATIONAL BUILDINGS RECORD, London, 50 (and the late F. H. Crossley), 51; NATIONAL GALLERY, London, 41, 328, 391; NATIONAL GALLERY OF ART, Washington, 194, 349; NATIONAL MARITIME MUSEUM, Greenwich, Cover, Pls. VI, VII, X, XII, XVIII, and 92, 93, 121, 193, 221, 248, 314, 407; NATIONAL PORTRAIT GALLERY, London, 65, 70, 102, 111, 112, 117, 129, 131, 132, 134–6, 145, 146, 148, 152, 154, 155, 160–1, 167, 168, 189, 228, 233, 238, 240–3, 245, 246, 249, 255, 257, 258, 265, 268, 270, 272, 280–3, 289, 290, 297, 303, 304, 308–10, 313, 315, 316, 327, 364, 372, 378, 381, 382, 398, 402–4, 411, 460, 461, 465, 466, 475, 479, 484, 491, 523, 524, 551, 553, 554; NATIONAL TRUST, London, 325; NEW YORK HISTORICAL SOCIETY, 197, 198, 210, 216, 223, 438; NEW YORK STATE HISTORICAL ASSOCIATION, Cooperstown, N.Y., 449; NEW YORK PUBLIC LIBRARY, 211, 213, 332, 335, 341, 345, 365, 367, 369, 501; HIS GRACE THE DUKE OF NORTHUMBERLAND, 98, 178; ODHAMS PRESS, Pl. XXII; EARL OF ONSLOW, 302; PAN-ASIA PHOTOS, 590; PARKER GALLERY, London, Pls. XIV, XVII, XX and 5, 374, 409, 470; PEABODY MUSEUM, Salem, Mass., 3; PENNSYLVANIA ACADEMY OF FINE ARTS, 333; PENNSYLVANIA HISTORICAL SOCIETY, 219, 220, 338, 339; PHAIDON PRESS, London (from *The Bayeux Tapestry*, edited by Sir Frank Stenton, 1957), Pl. I, and 15–22; PIERPONT MORGAN LIBRARY, New York, 1, 28, 87; PILGRIM HALL, Plymouth, Mass., 196; PIX PHOTOS LTD. (G. F. Allen), 103, 262, 321; PLANET NEWS, 573; HIS GRACE THE DUKE OF PORTLAND, 120; ENOCH PRATT FREE LIBRARY, Baltimore, 217; PRINCETON UNIVERSITY LIBRARY, 348; QUEEN'S COLLEGE, Cambridge, 69; RADIO TIMES HULTON PICTURE LIBRARY, 72, 123–5, 135, 151, 199, 362, 415, 500, 528, 529, 533, 535, 536, 543, 545–8, 552, 557, 558, 560, 564, 565, 570, 571, 574–6, 579–80, 591, 593; P. A. REUTER, 563; HIS GRACE THE DUKE OF RICHMOND AND GORDON, 229, 301, 390; THE RIJKSMUSEUM, Amsterdam, 247, 261; ESTATE OF FREDERICK H. RINDGE, on loan to Museum of Fine Arts, Boston, 357; ABBY ALDRICH ROCKEFELLER FOLK ART COLLECTION, Williamsburg, Virginia, 346; ROYAL ACADEMY OF ARTS, London, 400; ROYAL COMMISSION ON HISTORICAL MONUMENTS, London, 23; CITY ART MUSEUM, St Louis, Missouri, 433; MARQUESS OF SALISBURY, 127; MAJOR THE HON. PETER SAMUEL, 395; LORD SANDYS, 171; SCIENCE MUSEUM, London, 412; WALTER SCOTT (Bradford), 32, 33, 82; SCOTTISH NATIONAL PORTRAIT GALLERY, 119, 166; J. FOWLER SMITH, Salisbury, 218; SOCIETY OF ANTIQUARIES OF LONDON, 286; SIR JOHN SOANE'S MUSEUM, 298, 306; EARL SPENCER, Pls. XI, XV, and 244, 271 (Photo, Mrs M. I. Webb); CAPTAIN E. G. C. SPENCER-CHURCHILL, 319; LAWRENCE STONE, Oxford, 8, 14, 63, 79, 90; TATE GALLERY, London, 329, 389, 414; THAMES & HUDSON (from *English Parish Churches*, by Graham Hutton and Edwin Smith), 84; BARON THYSSEN, Lugano, Pl. IV; THE TIMES, 287, 288; DR G. M. TREVELYAN, 483; TRINITY COLLEGE, Cambridge, 29; UNITED STATES INFORMATION SERVICES, London, Pls. XXI, XXIII, and 203, 204, 343, 344, 347, 417, 424, 443, 451, 454, 499, 502, 505, 506, 515, 519, 530, 531, 568, 569, 572, 578, 596–8, 601; RALPH BRUCE VERNEY, ESQ., 173, 476; VICTORIA AND ALBERT MUSEUM, London, Pls. XVI, XIX, and 27, 47, 91, 150, 175, 269, 326, 376, 385, 410, 467, 468; WALLACE COLLECTION, London, 115; LORD WALPOLE, 322; WASHINGTON UNIVERSITY, St Louis, Missouri, 439; WARBURG INSTITUTE, London, 25, 26, 31, 38, 46, 264, 266, 284; EARL OF WARWICK (and Radio Times Hulton Picture Library), Pl. V; HAROLD WHITE and PITKIN PICTORIALS LTD., 100, 101; REECE WINSTONE, Bristol, 9, 49, 140, 158, 164, 170, 251, 254, 263, 274, 277, 388, 406; G. BERNARD WOOD, Rawdon, Leeds, 7, 81; WORCESTER COLLEGE, Oxford, 224, 225; JOHN WYNDHAM, ESQ., 97.

The remainder of the pictures are the property of the magazine *History Today*.

1 **MEDIEVAL WARFARE:** a picture from the 'Life of St Edmund' (1125–50)

2　Detail from a representation of **THE FIELD OF THE CLOTH OF GOLD** where Henry VIII met the King of France in June 1520, amid glittering pageantry and ceremonial jousts

Introduction

Nearly nine hundred years ago, a group of craftsmen—who, it is now thought, may have been Anglo-Saxon artists—joined forces to produce a masterpiece unequalled since the collapse of the Roman Empire. On a strip of linen, two hundred and thirty feet long but only twenty inches wide, they embroidered a pictorial narrative of the recent conquest of England, showing the coronation of the last Anglo-Saxon monarch and his earlier fateful meeting with Duke William of Normandy: William laying his plans to cross the Channel and occupy the English throne: the invasion itself and the hard-fought battle that followed: finally, the death of King Harold, struck down in the thick of the fray among his nobles and his house carls, who, as soon as their leader has fallen, break and run before the Norman knights. The Bayeux Tapestry, however, is not merely an artistic triumph: it is also an ambitious attempt to tell an historical story with the help of pictures, so that we gain a cumulative impression of the dramatic sweep of great events, as the eye travels rapidly on from episode to episode.

Nine sections of the famous tapestry are represented in the opening section of the present book. They provide the reader with an extraordinarily vivid glimpse of life at the beginning of the feudal period; and at the same time they may help to explain the method employed by the editors of this pictorial survey. *The Past We Share* is not an illustrated history, so much as an historical panorama, in which pictures have been assembled to form a continuous frieze, with passages of text, where the basic story requires elucidation. For the most part, however, the plates selected, with their captions, are allowed to tell their own tale; which they do both by conveying information—about

3 **AN AMERICAN PLANTER SELLS HIS TOBACCO; from a 'Map of Virginia', 1775**

the physical appearance of men and women during such-and-such an age, the customs they practised and the buildings they inhabited—and by evoking the general atmosphere of the period, its background of ideas and feelings.

We watch, for example, the roughness and sternness of Norman rule, exemplified in the castles that the Normans raised and the cathedrals that they built and decorated, merging gradually into the more graceful and homely civilization of the thirteenth and the fourteenth centuries. Next, we observe the decline of feudalism; and, confronted with photographs of a Gloucestershire 'wool church' and a company of wool-merchants' fine half-timbered hall, we become aware of the prosperous development of the English middle classes. Later again, when Henry VIII has abolished the monasteries and decisively broken away from Rome, his character and the characters of the 'New Men' who surrounded him are reflected in a series of brilliant individual portraits. Holbein furnishes an impressive array of hard, resolute, unsmiling masks—the land-grabbing *parvenus* who founded their fortunes upon the ruins of the old order. Turn the page, and their descendants emerge, clad in Elizabethan finery—courtiers, soldiers and politicians, still devoted to the pursuit of power and profit, but learning to cultivate the arts and the graces of life.

Almost simultaneously, we get our first view of a fabulous continent beyond the Atlantic Ocean; and another story begins to unfold, which for more than two hundred years remains closely connected with the story of the British Isles. But, as English settlers oust the primitive tribesmen depicted in early books of travel, and fortified settlements

4 **AN EIGHTEENTH-CENTURY PICNIC, held by nature-loving visitors to the Farne Islands**

are replaced by busy, well-built Georgian cities, we meet, among contemporary portraits of the Founding Fathers and their wives and
children, faces that are typically *American* and bear strangely little resemblance to their less adventurous cousins overseas. The spirit of
independence that these faces reveal soon has momentous political
results; a random shot is fired at Lexington; civil strife explodes in
armed conflict; and the two stories we have been following suddenly
cease to run along parallel lines. Henceforward the only links that
unite the British and American peoples are the recollection of their
common past and the ideas they have inherited.

That past is our subject—a subject of particular significance in the
troubled post-war age. However remote its early periods may seem,
they witnessed the birth of beliefs and institutions that continue to
flourish at the present day. Thus Magna Carta, although issued during
the reign of King John, at the beginning of the thirteenth century, first
outlined that ideal of individual freedom—of the rights of the ordinary
citizen to life, liberty and the pursuit of happiness—which is still
upheld and defended in Great Britain and in the United States.
Similarly, the struggle between King and Parliament that produced the
English Civil Wars helped to shape the institutions of modern parliamentary government. Even the political contests of the English
eighteenth century, at a time when the power of the Crown seemed to
encroach upon the power of the Commons, played an important part
in the education of the two great English-speaking peoples. At least
until the beginning of the nineteenth century, they were peoples of
largely the same blood—Saxon and Norman, with Scottish, Welsh and

5 **NEW YORK IN THE 'SEVENTIES;** scene on the Terrace in Central Park

Irish infiltrations; and they had inherited both the same conception of justice—the equality of all men before the law—and the same attitude towards the idea of government: when the American Colonists refused to accept taxation without representation, they were voicing a point of view held by their seventeenth-century English ancestors. The two countries possess, moreover, a common intellectual climate. For over two hundred years, English writers have been eagerly read in the United States; and, during a comparatively recent period, the new American literature was not yet studied as a separate course in trans-atlantic schools.

So much for the volume's scope; our editorial method we have already discussed. Now we must say something about the principles that have governed our selection of pictures. Except in very rare instances, all are of contemporary origin. King John and the signing of Magna Carta are not illustrated by a Victorian artist's imaginative version of what he believed *might* have happened when the rebellious barons met at Runnymede. Instead, we give a photograph of the royal seal that was attached to the bottom of the parchment sheet, and a second photograph of the King's sepulchral statue, with its fierce, choleric head, executed, no doubt, by a sculptor who had studied the features of the living man.

In gathering illustrations, we have thrown our net as widely as possible. Here are portraits, sculptured or painted: reproductions of drawings and illuminated manuscripts: broadsheets and satirical prints: contemporary pictures of historical scenes: photographs of cathedrals, churches, houses, and representative specimens of the

6 **CHURCHILL, ROOSEVELT, STALIN at the Yalta Conference, February 1945**

various arts and crafts. To the architectural productions of an age we attach particular value. Historical processes have few more eloquent memorials than the buildings that they leave behind. For, although the language of written history is sometimes ambiguous, and the same set of recorded facts may be capable of several different interpretations, no one who studied a Norman keep could fail to understand what Norman Rule, after 1066, meant to the conquered English people, or how King William enforced the system of taxation outlined in the Domesday Book. Similarly, the spirit of sixteenth-century England is brought home to us by a picture of an Elizabethan mansion; while the English Augustan Age, with its prosperity and its love of dignity and elegance, comes alive again in any photograph of one of Robert Adam's houses.

To provide a balanced presentation, nevertheless, has always been the editors' aim. Besides a drawing or a photograph of a house, we have here and there placed a portrait of the person who inhabited it; and at the same time we have tried to suggest the kind of daily life that he and his family led, the faith that inspired them and the beliefs and the political theories they held. The effect is intended to be panoramic; and we suggest that, before he examines the captions, a reader should allow his eye to rove across a whole section, thus gaining a general picture of the age, which, at a later stage, he can amplify and enrich by referring to the letterpress. Thus he may gradually arrive at a comprehensive view, which here covers nine centuries in the evolution of the English-speaking peoples. To those peoples, their past and their future, its editors dedicate this book.

Plate I   **The BAYEUX TAPESTRY**, embroidered not long after the Battle of Hastings, commem-
orates William the Conqueror's victory and gives the Norman view of the course of events that led up
to it.   In the scene (*above*) English foot-soldiers, armed with heavy battle-axes, confront Norman
knights amid the hail of arrows that doomed the Anglo-Saxon kingdom

THE
NORMAN KINGDOM
1066-1216

For the first and last time in almost a thousand years of history, during the autumn of 1066, England was invaded by an aggressive continental power, and the army who manned its defences was defeated and driven from the field. At Hastings, King Harold fell, and the Anglo-Saxon race came under foreign domination. Simultaneously, an issue was decided that helped to shape the whole future of the English-speaking peoples. Should England take her place in the Latin civilization of Western and Southern Europe? Or should she cast in her lot with the Scandinavian kingdoms of the North? The Duke of Normandy, William the Conqueror, was by descent a Norseman; but by tastes and training he belonged to France. And, although the society that he overthrew was no less highly developed than his own, the Anglo-Saxon realm was politically weak; whereas Duke William commanded the support of a disciplined and well-knit feudal system. Into that system England was incorporated after a brief but savage struggle.

William's expeditionary force—a fleet of some seven hundred ships, carrying an army of about seven thousand men—had set sail across the Channel on September 27. Next day, with his knights, men-at-arms and archers, he landed at Pevensey in Sussex. North and South the rival forces assembled. Edward the Confessor, that pious but ineffective sovereign, who, according to William, had once promised him the English Crown, had died on January 5, 1066; and he had been succeeded by Harold, son of Earl Godwin of Essex, Edward's former minister. Brave, experienced and energetic, Harold knew that he must fight for the throne he had inherited; and his first task was to repel another body of invaders, the Norsemen, who had landed that summer in Yorkshire. Having routed them at the battle of Stamford Bridge, fought on September 25, he received news of the second invasion and immediately marched southwards. In mid-October, at Hastings, he came face to face with William's armoured line.

7 A Norman DOOR-KNOCKER in the great northern Cathedral of Durham, grotesque but awe-inspiring

There, above the town, a desperate conflict took place on October 14. The English foot-soldiers, wielding heavy battle-axes, proved no match for William's archers and his fifteen hundred mounted men. But the English put up a fierce resistance; and they were not swept from the field until Harold and his brothers had fallen in the thick of the fight. Then, leaderless, they turned to flee. Having made a circular sweep around the English capital, William entered London and was crowned at Westminster on Christmas Day.

Norman rule

8 SAMSON, his long hair curving back in a mane, wrestles with the jaws of a lion. A twelfth-century relief at Stretton Sugwas, Herefordshire

Castles and churches are the surviving monuments of Norman rule in England, where a few thousand French soldiers and clerics now held all positions of power. The loosely-knit fabric of the Anglo-Saxon kingdom was reorganized by its conqueror on firmly authoritarian and severely feudal lines; the imposition of the feudal system meant that every man must have his master, and every master must swear to serve the King in war. William I, a merciless tax-collector, had the whole country carefully surveyed, so that he knew the exact value and ownership of every acre of his realm; the results of this survey were recorded in Domesday Book. But the institutions of the Anglo-Saxons in law and government were adopted by the new rulers; the setting up of the Norman kingdom did not involve a complete break with the Anglo-Saxon past. The blending of Saxon and Norman traditions had already begun.

The Conqueror left the kingdom to his second son, William, surnamed Rufus or the Red, who proved an even more ferocious and exacting monarch than his father. Slain by an arrow while hunting in the New Forest, he was succeeded by his brother Henry, the first of the great royal law-givers. During the opening decades of the twelfth century, Henry I laid the foundation of orderly government that was to remain unshaken by later civil wars.

Henry II and Becket

After a period of anarchy and confusion, during which the Norman barons made war among one another as they pleased, Henry II, grandson of Henry I, came to the throne in 1154. By birth he was Count of Anjou, by inheritance Duke of Normandy, by marriage the feudal overlord of two-thirds of France. In his reign, which lasted until 1189, England formed only part of a great continental empire. Henry Plantaganet was a short, thick-set man of restless energy and furious

9 (opposite) A series of massive castles are the surviving symbols of Norman rule. ROCHESTER KEEP, dominating the Medway valley in Kent, was built for the baron Gundulf in 1077 on a site that the Romans and Saxons had fortified

temper. He exercised a very real authority. His court was perpetually on the move, as he travelled widely across his many dominions.

During Henry's lifetime, Europe was distracted by the problem of the relationship between Church and State. Which of them held the ultimate power? Henry himself, having appointed his faithful follower, Thomas Becket, Archbishop of Canterbury, was astonished and enraged to discover that the new head of the English Church stood for religious privileges against the King. At Henry's instigation, Becket was murdered in his own cathedral on December 29, 1170.

Richard Coeur de Lion, Crusader

While the Normans consolidated their kingdom in England, Europe had been aroused by a call to liberate the Holy Places of Palestine from infidel rule. In 1099 the knights of the First Crusade had captured Jerusalem and set up a chain of principalities on the coast of the Levant. At the end of the next century these states were again falling one by one into the hands of Islam. A new Crusade set out in 1190 to rescue them. Its most heroic leader was Richard Coeur de Lion, son of Henry II. By hard fighting the Crusader states were re-established, though Jerusalem remained undelivered. On his way home, Richard fell into the hands of his enemy, Leopold of Austria, and was for long held prisoner in Germany. In his reign of eleven years, this romantic warrior spent only six months in England.

King John and Magna Carta

King John, Henry II's younger son, came of fierce and unruly stock. Believing that the 'state was himself', he extorted money to suit his personal convenience and violated the established customs of feudal society according to his own pleasure. By doing so, he antagonized not only his powerful barons, but the lesser gentry and the townspeople; and in 1215, on the little island of Runnymede in the Thames, his barons eventually brought him to book and forced him to seal Magna Carta, the most important document in English constitutional history. It began by reaffirming the feudal rights of the barons. But although Magna Carta is, in some parts, reactionary, and in others, rather vaguely worded, it contained at last a general statement of the privileges of the ordinary citizen, from which were afterwards derived such fruitful conceptions as that of *Habeas Corpus* and the right to trial by jury. Re-interpreted by successive generations, Magna Carta became the guarantee, under law, of the freedom of the individual. A year after the signing of Magna Carta, John died; and his young son, King Henry III, succeeded to the English throne.

A crux in the struggle between Church and State was reached in the martyrdom of St Thomas Becket in 1170. 10 (*left, top*) **The Archbishop excommunicates sinners, and conducts an altercation with the Kings of England and France.** 11 (*left, bottom*) **Becket is warned not to risk danger by returning from exile to England. There the five knights 12 (*right*), on the King's hasty orders, murder him in his own Cathedral, a crime that horrified the King when he heard of it**

13 **MAGNA CARTA, sealed in 1215, was the first English contract of State between sovereign and subjects that attempted to safeguard individual rights. THE GREAT SEAL OF KING JOHN was attached to the Charter agreed at Runnymede. The fiery, bellicose, thwarted John** 14 (*below*) **lies in effigy at Worcester Cathedral**

The Bayeux Tapestry

Designed and executed probably by Anglo-Saxon artists at the direction of the Conqueror's half-brother, Bishop Ode of Bayeux, who appears to have commissioned it for his new cathedral, the Bayeux Tapestry tells the story of the campaign in a two-hundred-and-thirty-foot frieze of extraordinarily graphic scenes

15 Harold, touching two shrines, is tricked into swearing allegiance at Bayeux to William Duke of Normandy, who looks on from his throne

16 Despite his oath, Harold allows himself to be crowned King of England; he shows himself to the people, flanked by two nobles and Stigant, Archbishop of Canterbury

17 During the spring and summer of 1066 craftsmen fell trees in the Norman woods to build the dragon-headed ships that will bear the Conqueror's army across the Channel

18 William's fleet, bearing about seven thousand men and perhaps two thousand war-horses, approaches the hostile English coast behind protective barriers of large shields

19 Having landed and established a camp, the Norman invaders prepare their first meal; a fire blazes beneath a military cauldron and the cooks serve bread and meat

20 Carrying shields, spears and battle-axes, the Anglo-Saxon infantry stand up to the fierce onrush of the Norman knights and the first attack is repulsed

21 Ponderous battle-axes bring down the Norman horses, as cavalrymen, wielding their swords, hurl themselves against the foot-soldiers; the action lasted for eight hours

22 Towards evening on October 14, Harold is killed and the battle is over. It is now thought that the falling figure, struck by a broad-bladed Norman sword, represents the Anglo-Saxon King

Craftsmen in stone

25 The severity of Norman workmanship was soon modified by intense religious feeling. This dramatic head of CHRIST RAISING LAZARUS in Chichester Cathedral, belongs to the second quarter of the twelfth century

26 At the opening of the thirteenth century, sculptors first became aware of the beauty and dignity of the human face. HEAD OF ST JOHN, of about 1200-10, at St. Mary's Abbey, York

24 The northern wing of the transept of WINCHESTER CATHEDRAL, a splendid example of Norman-Romanesque building, was begun in 1079. The Conqueror, who regarded the city as his second capital, celebrated his second coronation there

23 (opposite) Norman architects softened the effect of their massive round-headed arches with bands of rich and elaborate Romanesque ornament. This door of an English parish church, at Kilpeck, Herefordshire, dates from about 1095-1150

16

The graphic arts

28 **A famous school of draughtsmanship and illumination had flourished at Winchester since Anglo-Saxon times. Among its other triumphs, it produced these graphic illustrations of THE STORY OF DAVID**

29 **A monkish artist, the SCRIBE EADWINE, to judge by his name a man of Anglo-Saxon descent, was employed at Canterbury about 1150 to design and illuminate a psalter. His expressive self-portrait shows the scribe at his desk**

30 **RICHARD COEUR DE LION, Crusader, one of the Conqueror's most martial descendants, who ruled the kingdom from 1189 to 1199, is represented on this tile made to decorate the pavement of Chertsey Abbey**

27 (*opposite*) **The influence of Byzantine artists can be seen in glass-painting of the late twelfth century: for example, in this splendid figure of METHUSELAH, which looks down on worshippers at Canterbury Cathedral**

II

THE AGE OF CHIVALRY

31 John's successor, **HENRY III**, who had inherited his father's waywardness and unpredictable disposition, ruled the kingdom from 1216 to 1272. The new Westminster Abbey, whence this head comes, is his most enduring monument

The age of chivalry was an age of warfare. Much of the thirteenth century was filled with civil strife, King against barons, knight against knight. Yet during the long reign of King Henry III, which lasted for fifty-six years, some of the foundations of English political development were tentatively laid. The king himself was of wayward, impetuous character, more consistently absorbed in such projects as the rebuilding of Westminster Abbey—which remains his memorial—than in the arts and problems of government. It fell to others to leave their stamp on the political structure of England. In the efforts of the barons to curb the powers of the Crown, and the attempts of the Crown to defend itself, the outstanding leader was Simon de Montfort, around whose name in later centuries was to gather a legend of popular English leadership that would have surprised him. By birth a Frenchman, de Montfort was in England Earl of Leicester, a great magnate and brother-in-law to the King. For many years one of the King's principal advisers and lieutenants, the Earl passed, upon a sudden quarrel, into armed opposition. Defeating his sovereign in the field, he made himself for a short time master of England. He met his end in 1265, slain in battle by the King's son, Edward, who rallied to

32 and 33 **All the human charm and decorative refinement of ENGLISH THIRTEENTH-CENTURY SCULPTURE characterize these two benign angels above separate arches in Westminster Abbey, from where they have looked down on centuries of ceremonial**

his support the many baronial interests that the Earl had in his turn offended.

The birth of Parliament

In his lifetime, however, de Montfort had helped to create, perhaps unwittingly, an institution that gradually grew strong enough to mould the course of British history—that is, Parliament. All over Europe during the Middle Ages, Estates of the realm were emerging, whose power lay in their right to grant the Crown taxes and to beg for the redress of their grievances before they did so. In its origins the English Parliament did not differ greatly from its European counterparts, but comparatively early in its life it came to be accepted as a customary part of the royal system of rule. Over the centuries, it gained in authority, until the time came when it could successfully challenge the Crown itself. In most other countries the Estates dwindled away or fell into abeyance, but in England the Parliamentary tradition slowly fortified itself and matured to the point where it could serve as a model of consultative government for much of the rest of the world.

In the thirteenth century this course of evolution lay far in the future, but the Parliaments of Henry III's reign mark its beginnings.

For de Montfort, the assembly of notables, to which were added representative knights from the shires and burgesses from the towns, afforded simply one instrument among many in the pursuit of his aims. The purpose of the so-called 'great' Parliament, summoned by him in January 1265, was to give an air of legality to his seizure of power, and to pass the laws that he required of it. It was after his death that a remarkable development occurred; then his vanquisher, Edward, recognizing the usefulness of Parliament as a law-making body, adapted it to his own designs. When Edward came to the throne, and embarked upon a period of resourceful royal rule, he decided to associate Parliament with most of his major enactments. The notion was thus born of a law-giving sovereign habitually functioning through the means of Parliament and with its aid. It was a notion as yet perhaps only dimly apprehended, and a great distance had to be travelled before Parliament itself claimed even a share in sovereign power; but by the time of the death of King Edward I, the important initial step had been taken.

The British Isles

In the eyes of his subjects, a mediaeval monarch was hedged with some divinity, but he was expected to show himself worthy of his divine right. A firm hand at home and success in foreign wars were essential qualifications for respect and fame. The two requirements went together, since a vigorous king, gifted with abilities as a warrior, naturally looked beyond his boundaries for means of displaying his power and occupying the ambitions of his barons. His own immediate aim might be the conquest of territory, or the replenishing of his

34 **Unlike the majority of English Gothic cathedrals, SALISBURY belongs to a single period. It was planned and completed within a space of about forty years—between 1220 and 1260**

Exchequer by tribute or ransom, but one certain effect of a well-organized campaign abroad was the enhancement of the authority of the Crown.

The reign of Edward I, and much of his grandson's, Edward III, were assertive periods of this kind. For an English monarch of the later Middle Ages there were two main fields for military expansion. One lay across the Channel in France—the main target of Edward III—and the other at home within the British Isles. It was an attempt to impose a unity upon the isles that chiefly pre-occupied King Edward I. To him belongs the distinction of formally bringing Wales under the English Crown—not without fierce resistance on the part of the Welsh —and of creating his son the first English Prince of Wales. Over Ireland, like his predecessors since Henry II, Edward claimed sovereignty, although, in fact, the English writ ran only in the neighbourhood of Dublin known as the Pale; beyond it the Irish septs pursued their immemorial customs. With Scotland there was a long struggle, and Edward has passed down to history, rather dubiously, as 'the hammer of the Scots'. At first, there seemed a chance that he would attain his ends peacefully. When the last Scottish king of the old line perished by riding his horse over a cliff on a dark night, the throne fell to his infant grand-daughter Margaret, the Maid of Norway. A royal marriage between the Scottish heiress and Edward's son and heir seemed a glittering possibility. The conjunction of the Crowns, however, was not to be achieved by the union of dynasties for another three centuries. Margaret died on the journey from Norway, and at once the Scottish succession fell into dispute. King Edward seized the oppor-

35 **As in Norman times, castle and cathedral dominated the landscape side by side. CAERNARVON CASTLE was begun by Edward I about 1284 to hold down the subjugated Welsh**

36 **The effeminate offspring of a warrior king,
EDWARD II (1307-27) ruled through a succession of unworthy favourites and finally met a
frightful death. Head of his alabaster effigy in
Gloucester Cathedral**

37 **Into the pattern of religious sym-
bolism, medieval illuminators wove
their exuberant fancies. A detail from
the ORMSBY PSALTER (c. 1310-25)**

tunity to support one of the candidates, while placing him in the
position of a vassal. His harsh exactions aroused the patriotism of the
Scots which could not be quenched by Edward's victorious arms. Their
national leader, William Wallace, was eventually captured and hanged
at Tyburn, but within a decade a terrible vengeance fell upon the
English. At Bannockburn, a large English army, commanded by
Edward's feckless son and successor, was shattered and crushed by the
Scots under Robert Bruce. Scottish independence was henceforth
assured. For more than two hundred years, border warfare flickered
between the two countries, flaring now and again into a full-scale campaign. Under the two Bruce kings, and their heirs, the Stuarts, England's difficulties were Scotland's opportunity, and the 'auld alliance'
between Scotland and France became a frequent cause of English
anxiety.

Edward I, a warrior to the end, had died in a litter at the head of his
army. His son met a melancholy fate. After a reign dominated alter-
nately by court favourites and turbulent barons, he was brutally murdered in Berkeley Castle on the orders of his wife's lover.

The Wars with France

English relations with France had been close, complex and often hostile, ever since William of Normandy had gained the English throne.
By the late thirteenth century, the Conqueror's duchy, and many other

Plate II (*opposite*) **The thirteenth century, an age of faith, was also an age of incessant warfare,
when the king clashed with his feudal vassals and knight contended against knight. The ideals of
chivalry did not preclude savage brutality and rapacity. Pen-drawing of a CRUSADER, mid-
thirteenth century**

French territories which had formed part of the Henry II's continental empire, were lost to the Crown of England. But there remained the considerable feoff of Aquitaine, centred in Bordeaux, which the English kings held as vassals of the French. For a sovereign to hold part of his lands as a subordinate to another was not unusual in the days before the existence of national states, but it was frequently a source of dispute. Aquitaine could be a flash-point whenever the French or English monarch chose. There were others, including a claim to the French throne advanced by Edward III, and nominally maintained by all his successors until George III relinquished it at the Treaty of Amiens concluded with Napoleon in 1802. More important to the countrymen of England was the wool-trade with Flanders. Wool was England's chief export and her main source of wealth. The towns of Flanders provided the market for it, and English governments needed to preserve Flanders from French encroachment. Honour and the claims of chivalry thus went hand in hand with economic interests. And so, for many mixed reasons, the long wars with France began.

King Edward I had campaigned with success against the French in Flanders. His grandson achieved far more spectacular feats. A naval victory at Sluys gave Edward III command of the English Channel, which, not for the last time in the course of centuries, was to be vital for the success of the kingdom's arms. Six years later, in 1346, King Edward invaded Normandy, marched on Paris, beat a retreat towards the Channel ports, and, in the course of it, won the overwhelming victory of Crécy. Here for the first time the English long-bowmen effectively displayed their skill and firepower—archery had become a national sport. Before Edward left France, the port of Calais was captured in a famous siege, and remained an English garrison town and outlet for trade until the unfortunate reign of Queen Mary Tudor. In 1558 it was the last English possession in France to revert to the French. From Aquitaine, meanwhile, in the decade that followed Crécy, King Edward's son, named the Black Prince, after the colour of his armour, made armed forays and fought fierce battles that resulted in the capture of the French king and the recognition of English sovereignty over an extensive Aquitaine. The power of England had reached one of its heights; some depths, and more heights, were to follow.

England takes shape

Edward III and his sons, whose state and grandeur he carefully endowed, lent lustre to the Age of Chivalry. He and his family were lovers of the tournament and all forms of pageantry. Perhaps the apogee of the age was the foundation of the Order of the Garter in 1348 after

38 **EDWARD III** (1327-77) revived the militant tradition of his grandfather Edward I, hammered the Scots and embarked on the long series of campaigns against France known as the Hundred Years War. Portrait head in Westminster Abbey

39 (*below*) The son of Edward III, **EDWARD THE BLACK PRINCE** (1330-76), so-called because he wore black armour, spent much of his life abroad carrying on his father's ambitious French wars. Gilt copper effigy in Canterbury Cathedral

40 **The Annunciation and John the Baptist, from an ivory panel known as the 'GRANDISSON IVORY', executed about 1335-45 for the Bishop of Exeter**

42 (*left*) **In 1381, the hard-pressed English peasantry rose against their feudal overlords. JOHN BALLE meets the King's troops at the head of his insurgent followers.** 43 (*right*) **RICHARD RIDES OUT TO MEET THE PEOPLE, and Wat Tyler, another champion of the peasants, is struck down and slain by the Lord Mayor. These miniatures illustrate a manuscript of the Chronicles of Jean Froissart (1337-1410)**

the sovereign's return from his triumphs in France. The King had promised to create an Order of the Knights of the Round Table, such as the legendary King Arthur had led. In a festivity at Calais to celebrate the capture of the town, the celebrated incident occurred in which the young Countess of Salisbury, with whom the King was in love, dropped her garter during a dance with him. He picked it up and bound it round his knee, rebuking the mockery of onlookers with the words that were to become famous as the motto of the Order: '*Honi soit qui mal y pense*' (shame to him with evil thoughts). The blue garter became the emblem of this highly exclusive order of chivalry, which united the King and his sons and his principal barons and knights in a personal bond of brotherhood.

Thus was symbolized the gallantry of the age; but beneath the brilliant surface more sombre events were unrolling. In the same year as the Order of the Garter was founded, England was swept by the first visitation of the bubonic plague, known as the Black Death. During the next three decades, the plague recurred at intervals, taking a heavy toll in lives and causing widespread misery in town and country alike. The growing prosperity of England suffered a setback, and out of the discontents of the time arose movements of social revolution that confronted the government of Edward's grandson and successor with sharp and severe crises. There was a period of unrest and rebellion, the leaders of which were ruthlessly eliminated, although their ideas—not

41 (*opposite*) **Attended by his patron saints against a background of delicately stippled gold, RICHARD II (1377-99) kneels in prayer before the Virgin and the Infant Christ. The Wilton Diptych (1380-90?), of which this is the left-hand leaf, is one of the earliest masterpieces of original English painting**

44   Greatest of English poets before the appearance of Shakespeare, GEOFFREY CHAUCER (c. 1340-1400), an industrious civil servant, probably began the composition of the CANTERBURY TALES about 1387. Portrait from a manuscript of the early fifteenth century

yet of equality between men, but at least a fairer equity—were largely diffused and helped to influence the gradual transition from semi-feudal society to the age of the Renaissance and Reformation.

Amid these turmoils a recognizable England was taking shape. A new age of building began, in which farm-houses and town-houses, churches and bridges, were more important and numerous in construction than castles and fortresses. The first surviving portrait of an English monarch—Richard II—was painted. The first Bible in English was produced by the followers of the Church reformer, John Wyclif; and Geoffrey Chaucer, clerk of the King's works, justice of the peace, diplomatist and courtier, wrote the first great English poems, which provide a panorama of the kingdom's contemporary life. England had at last ceased to be Norman and was now distinctively English.

45   After RICHARD II's ARREST AT FLINT CASTLE, he was brought to London and deposed by Henry of Bolingbroke, the future Henry IV

46   The gilt copper HEAD OF RICHARD II, designed for his tomb at Westminster by Nicholas Broker and Godfrey Prest, suggests the romantic instability of his temperament

47   (opposite) Long flowing and gracefully undulating lines express the period's sense of beauty, and feminine fashions now become particularly attractive. Two WOODEN STATUES, about six feet high, today in Vicars Hall, Wells, Somerset

The thirteenth century . . . .

48 (*below*) **The fan-vault of the nave of EXETER CATHEDRAL is a triumph of the decorated style. Converging ribs of stone, which meet in circular bosses, produce a miraculous effect of lightness and solidity combined**

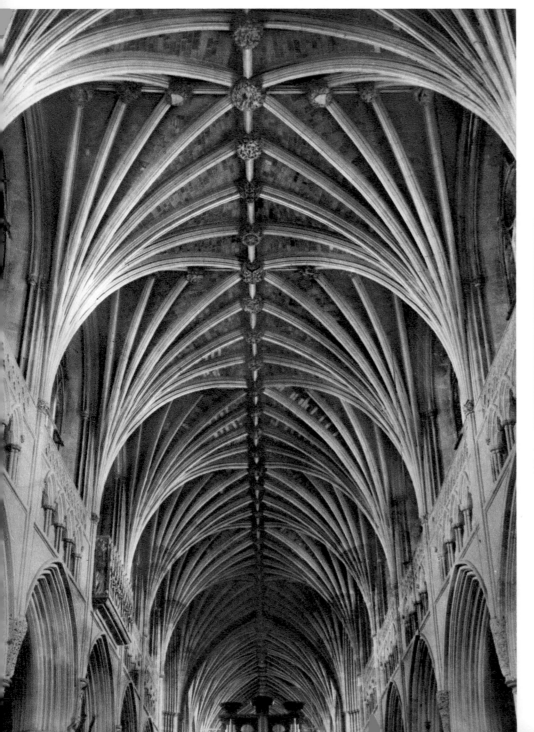

49 **At STOKESAY, Shropshire, stands an impressive example of an early English manor-house, which is half fortress and half private dwelling. The nearer southern tower dates from 1284**

. . . . and the fourteenth

51 Medieval sculptors adored the grotesque. Detail of an altar screen showing a BAGPIPER in Beverley Minster

50 The knight in a WINDOW AT TEWKES-BURY wears a surcoat, displaying his heraldic blazon, over the coat of chainmail that protects his body. But plate armour encases his arms and legs

52 The towers of BODIAM CASTLE are reflected in its broad moat. From a strategic point of view it is inconveniently sited. By 1386 the castle was becoming an object of aristocratic pride rather than a source of military strength

53 An extraordinary achievement of the medieval mason's skill are the four tremendous buttress arches that support the central bulk of WELLS CATHEDRAL. They were added in 1338

Work

and

play

54   **For the labouring masses it was a hard and difficult age. PEASANTS PLOUGH-ING, from the Luttrell Psalter, c. 1340**

55   **A MONK AND A LADY IN THE STOCKS: mid-fourteenth century**

56   **MESSENGER AND MONARCH: from the same manuscript**

57   **ARCHERY PRACTICE: from the Luttrell Psalter**

58　A GAME OF CHESS: from the four-teenth century 'Romance of Alexander'

59　A TRAINED HORSE: from the 'Romance of Alexander'

60　A PUPPET SHOW: from the 'Romance of Alexander'

61　THE BOWLING GREEN: from the 'Romance of Alexander'

62　A PERFORMING BEAR: from the 'Romance of Alexander'

THE

END

OF

FEUDALISM

63 Heads of the usurper **HENRY IV (1399-1413) AND HIS QUEEN,** from their tomb in Canterbury Cathedral

The House of Lancaster

As early as the thirteenth century, the strictly feudal relationships between the king, the barons and the commons had begun to change substantially, as facilities for the money motive ramified through the Kingdom. King Edward I's soldiers were no longer members of a feudal host, but paid archers and men-at-arms. Gradually the domains of great lords came to be held as sources of revenue rather than of feudal power; land was bought and sold; labour was rewarded in wages more often than in kind. At the same time, many merchant families were rising to affluence, some of them destined to form the ranks of a new nobility under the Tudors. This steady transformation of the social scene quickened in the fifteenth century, and was further hastened by the civil wars between the dynasties of Lancaster and York.

The House of Lancaster came to the throne by usurpation. Richard II, after years of tutelage under his royal uncles, had established a personal government that in the eyes of his more powerful subjects increasingly appeared tyrannical. When he attempted to confiscate the large estates of his cousin, Henry of Lancaster, he provoked an explosion. Henry, who was in exile, returned home, ostensibly to claim his inheritance, but in fact he seized the Crown. Richard was compelled to abdicate and Henry IV was acclaimed in his stead. The new King, a junior grandson of Edward III, owed his position to the use of force and the concurrence in his action of the Lords and Commons in Parliament. The direct line of succession had been balefully broken and

64   On St Crispin's Day, October 25, 1415, Henry V won at AGINCOURT one of the most resounding victories of the Hundred Years' War against France, when English archers, equipped with the long bow, routed the heavily armoured French cavalry. From a fifteenth-century manuscript

65   Not long after he had married the daughter of the French king and been adopted as her father's rightful heir, HENRY V (1413-22) died suddenly at the age of thirty-four while still campaigning on French territory

the Crown that he wore for the rest of his life remained uneasy on his head.

Upon this political scene of conspiracy and unrest there now strode a gifted, purposeful leader who threw the national energies of England into an ambitious war with France. Henry V, when Prince of Wales, had already shown his mettle as a soldier in defence of his father's Crown. Immediately upon his succession, he published his claim to the French throne, set on foot preparations for seizing it by conquest, and planned, when he had done so, to lead the joint arms of both countries in a crusade to regain Jerusalem. Henry's campaign led to one of the most famous victories in the annals of English arms. Agincourt was fought on the anniversary of St Crispin, October 25, 1415. Having landed in Normandy, and gained some local successes, Henry V repeated the manoeuvre of his great-grandfather, Edward III, and made for Calais. On his march the French caught up with him at Agincourt, near Boulogne, where the day was again won by a hail of English arrows. Five years later, the French king acknowledged Henry as his heir, and that fanatical warrior seemed to have France at his feet. Not long after his moment of triumph the King succumbed to an attack of dysentery, contracted during one of the numerous sieges of French towns with which warfare was now punctuated. He died in his thirty-fifth year, leaving his realms to a baby, nine months old. This infant grew up, as Henry VI, to be an amiable, pious figure, afflicted with periods of insanity, who presided during a long troubled reign over the dissolution of his continental empire, and at the moment of his death saw the extinction of his dynasty.

In France, the ablest of the King's uncles, John, Duke of Bedford, was his Regent. He was faced with the unrealizable task of imposing his sovereign's rule upon an increasingly recalcitrant nation, which was presently further rallied in patriotic spirit by the brief and miraculously successful military career of St Joan of Arc. Captured and charged with heresy, she was martyred at the stake in Rouen on May 29, 1431. Within a generation of her death, after long, wearisome and costly warfare, the English had lost every one of their French strongholds except Calais. The dream of a European empire, nourished over three centuries by the English House of Plantagenet, was now for all time ended.

The Wars of the Roses

In England, the King's government lay in the hands first of his uncle, Humphrey, Duke of Gloucester, who was more accomplished as a collector of books than in the arts of regency, and then in those of the Beaufort family, who were his cousins. Henry VI's own interests are commemorated in King's College, Cambridge, and in Eton, both of which he founded. In the country at large there was simultaneously discontent among the commons, vented in open rebellions, and lawlessness among the magnates which the régime, crippled by the burdens of the French war, was too lax and weak to control. All the motives for an outbreak of civil strife were accumulating. It came when the opposition party, led by the Duke of York, advanced in 1460 from demanding good government to claiming the throne itself. York, indeed, had a senior claim by female descent from Edward III. His name and that of the House of Lancaster now became rival symbols in the twenty-five years of intermittent disruption that followed. White and red roses came to be associated with the opposing sides and gave their name to the struggle. The actions of the Wars of the Roses were widely scattered, some being small local affairs, and only one or two of a broadly national character. They were marked by Yorkist triumph, a brief Lancastrian resurgence, and Yorkist victory again. In the course of them, a large proportion of the old nobility, and of the

67· Only son of Henry V, the pious, sickly, ineffective, **HENRY VI** (1422-61), here shown at prayer among his relations and nobles, lost his throne, and ten years later his life, during the long agony of the Wars of the Roses

66 After his death in the battle of Barnet, the **SEAL OF WARWICK THE KINGMAKER** (1428-71), greatest of contemporary war-lords, who had supported first the Yorkist, and then the Lancastrian party, was picked up on the bloodstained battlefield

royal family and its relations, were killed in battle or assassinated. The scene closes with the notorious murder of the young sons of the Yorkist King Edward IV—the Princes in the Tower—and the usurpation of their uncle, Richard III, himself slain upon the field of Bosworth in 1485 by the army of an obscure prince of Welsh descent with a tenuous Lancastrian ancestry, Henry Tudor.

The Middle Ages had gradually drawn to a close during the decades before Bosworth was fought. Feudalism was dead. The last glories of Gothic architecture in the perpendicular style were about to give place to novel modes in building. Caxton brought the art of printing to London, which was to open men's minds to fresh horizons, and eventually to change the whole relationship between government and governed. The Renaissance from Italy was about to spread to England and, under a new monarchy, fashion a new age.

68 **WILLIAM CAXTON** (c. 1422?-91), father of English printing, presents to his royal patron Edward IV, a copy of 'Dictes or Sayengis of the Philosophres', the first dated book printed in England

69 Edward IV (1461-70) contracted in 1464 a secret marriage with **ELIZA-BETH WOODVILLE.** The favouritism he showed his wife's family alienated many of the King's allies, including Warwick, the redoubtable Kingmaker

70 According to Tudor historians, it was **RICHARD III** (1483-85) who contrived the murder of the two young sons of Edward IV and Elizabeth Woodville. They met a sudden and mysterious death in (71) the **TOWER OF LONDON.** In 1485 Richard III was defeated by Henry Tudor and slain on the field of Bosworth

72   **Built by Richard II in 1399 as the central feature of his reconstructed palace, WESTMINSTER HALL, with its magnificent hammer-beam roof, was the scene of the King's own deposition. Here Charles I was later to be tried and sentenced**

73   **This richly sculptured SCREEN IN CANTERBURY CATHEDRAL illustrates the beginnings of the so-called Perpendicular style—more sumptuous, but less elegant than those of earlier centuries. Statues of Henry V, Richard II and Ethelbert**

Exteriors, interiors

74 As artillery grew more destructive, the castle lost its strategic value, and became a nobleman's fortified residence rather than a military strong-point. **HURSTMON-CEUX CASTLE**, built in 1440, has already begun to incorporate many of the comforts of an ordinary house

75 English commerce in the fifteenth century was still based upon the wool trade, and medieval cloth merchants enriched their native towns with churches and dignified secular buildings. The **GUILDHALL AT LAVENHAM** stands in the centre of the wool country

Gentleness

and

piety

76   This realistic self-portrait of JOHN SIFERWAS WITH HIS PATRON LORD LOVELL is thought to have been executed early in the reign of Henry IV. The artist was a Dominican friar and a famous illuminator of the day

77 (*below*)   A monk of Bury St Edmunds, JOHN LYDGATE (c. 1370-c. 1450) followed diligently in Chaucer's footsteps and, among his numerous poetic works, produced a supplement to the CANTERBURY TALES. Here he is depicted with the martial Earl of Salisbury

78   The precepts of the Christian faith continued to inspire medieval artists— painters and draughtsmen as well as sculptors and church-architects. These figures represent TRUTH, PURITY, HUMILITY AND POVERTY

79   Despite the widespread havoc wrought by the Wars of the Roses, they were fought out in a series of local conflicts, and religion and the arts of peace never ceased to hold their own. Effigy of ALICE, DUCHESS OF SUFFOLK at Ewelme, Oxfordshire

80 This exquisite ANNUNCIATION FROM
THE BEAUFORT HOURS is thought to
have been painted between 1401 and 1410. The
portraits are said to be of John Beaufort, Earl
of Somerset, and his wife Margaret de Holand

The glory of Gothic architecture

81   This impressive representation of
**KING DAVID PLAYING ON HIS
HARP** comes from the great east window of York Minster. It was created
during the first decade of the fifteenth
century by John Thornton of Coventry

82   The glass-painter's art had grown up
side by side with that of the illuminator.
Both told a religious story in luminous
colours and moving imagery. The **EAST
WINDOW AT YORK MINSTER** (1405-8)
illustrates the Apocalypse

83   Characteristic of English parish-churches, in regions where the wool-trade prospered, are elaborate and fantastic roofs over which a multitude of angels spread their wings. **ROOF AT MARCH, CAMBRIDGE**, a church built about 1450

84   One of the last important additions to **PETERBOROUGH CATHEDRAL**, founded as a monastery church in the seventh century, was this superb chapel, built towards the end of the feudal age, with its unequalled fan-vaulting

85   **CIRENCESTER CHURCH** in Gloucestershire is one of the 'wool-churches' raised by the rich merchants of fifteenth-century England. Observe the wealth of vertical lines from which the Perpendicular style derived its name

*The laws
of
peace and
war*

86 Justice is administered, during the
reign of Henry VI, at the COURT OF
THE KING'S BENCH. Five judges
preside; at the left are seated the members of the jury; prisoners await their
turn in chains

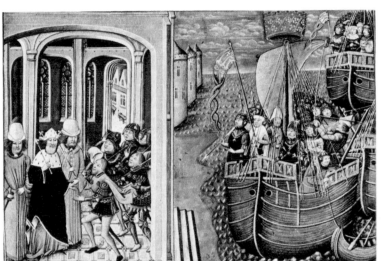

88 **ENGLISH SOLDIERS OF FORTUNE ARRIVE AT LISBON** to assist the King of Portugal. Companies of tough English mercenaries were employed by many English princes. This fifteenth-century picture shows an event that took place in 1385

89 **SIEGE WARFARE IN THE FIFTEENTH CENTURY** called for the use of many different weapons. Here artillerymen, bombarding the fortress, are supported by crossbow-men and a group of archers wielding long bows

90 Ten years before the outbreak of the Wars of the Roses, John Massingham and his assistants produced this gilt-copper effigy of **RICHARD, EARL OF WARWICK**—not to be confused with the Kingmaker, who bore the same title

87 (*left*) **THE TOURNAMENT**, at which gaudily caparisoned knights met to break their lances across a wooden barrier, long remained one of the most popular of aristocratic sports and pastimes. From **ORDINANCES OF CHIVALRY**, about 1470

THE
NEW
MONARCHY

91   **Henry VII (1485-1509), bust by Pietro Torrigiano**

The face of Henry Tudor wears a modern look. Shrewdness and foresight are stamped upon his features, and he was in fact the most accomplished businessman who ever held the English throne. Of obscure origins, King Henry VII, as he became, had risen through the slaughter of the War of the Roses to the supreme station. In his reign of twenty-four years, during which he survived many conspiracies, the foundations of the new monarchy were laid. After a generation of civil strife, orderly government was secured by his patience, persistence and good luck.

Henry VII was not himself an innovator, but his was an age of new ideas. The speculations of the Humanists reached England at this time, and Renaissance thought began to change and enliven long-accepted outlooks. Columbus made his celebrated voyage, and from Bristol in 1497 an expedition under John Cabot set out, financed by the King, which discovered Newfoundland and coasted the shores of the future New England. At home, a long-heralded new era was dawning. New men were rising, merchants, lawyers and churchmen, who took the place of the old nobility in the counsels of the Crown. New fashions in building, dress and manners gradually spread through the country. For the first time since the Black Death, the numbers of the population started to rise; trade and commerce flourished, and fresh horizons were everywhere opening. The beginning may be discerned of the great expansion in both physical and spiritual spheres that distinguished the English people of the sixteenth century. Over all presided an astute, watchful, calculating monarch. The glory and adventure that was to come in the Tudor epoch owe their origins to him.

Henry VIII and his Court

Henry VIII came to the throne at the age of eighteen, a gifted, glittering giant of a man, with a full treasury to call upon. His court in his early years was one of the gayest in Europe. The King was a passionate sportsman, a talented musician, a linguist, a theologian and a patron of arts and learning. The day-to-day work of governing his kingdom he left largely to his ministers, first the great Cardinal Wolsey, and then Thomas Cromwell.

But it was still an age of personal rule, and the King's character counted for much. Henry was imperious, wrathful and secretive. Not even the arrogant Cardinal at the height of his power could take royal favour for granted. No one could guess what designs Henry was meditating behind the formidable mask depicted by Holbein, with its small cruel mouth and small, widely separated eyes. On the European diplomatic stage the King played a conspicuous and imposing role. From his domestic circumstances came his misfortunes. His first wife,

92 (*left*) The first English landfall in the New World was made at Cape Breton Island by John Cabot, a native of Genoa, who sailed under the Tudor King's patronage. A ROUND SHIP of the period shows the kind of vessel in which he crossed the ocean. A north-east, as well as a north-west passage to the riches of the Indies was the hope of English adventurers. 93 John's son, SEBASTIAN CABOT, lived to become Governor of the English Muscovy Company in 1551

94   Lacking a male heir, and in fear of civil war after his death, Henry VIII was led to repudiate his wife and break with the Papacy in order to marry his mistress, ANNE BOLEYN (1507-36)

95   Tiring of Anne Boleyn's charms, the King turned his attentions to JANE SEYMOUR (1504-37), who bore him his much-desired son. Anne was executed; Jane died after childbirth. Their portraits are by Holbein

Catherine of Aragon, bore him no male heir. This disappointment provoked the quarrel with the Pope that led to England's break with Rome.

The Reformation

96   'One of the gayest courts in Europe': HENRY VIII WITH HIS JESTER

At Wittenberg in 1517 Martin Luther started a movement of protest within the Church that shortly engulfed all Europe. The Lutheran Reformation did not at first awaken many echoes in England, although it made its infiltrations. The crisis came when the King determined upon a divorce which the Pope refused to grant. Step by step, in order to marry Anne Boleyn, with whom he had fallen in love, Henry VIII was driven to the resolve to cast off all papal allegiance. Under the reforming influence of his Archbishop of Canterbury, Cranmer, the first full version of the Bible was published in English, and the Church of England began to take shape. Henry's matrimonial troubles were not ended by this religious transformation. He married four times again, and two of his wives met their death upon the block. Before her disgrace, Anne Boleyn gave birth to the most glorious of English rulers, the future Queen Elizabeth.

As Henry's reign drew on, Protestant doctrine began to secure a broader following in England. At the same time, the immemorial properties of the Church were confiscated by the State. The monasteries were suppressed and the extensive lands in their ownership sold

Plate IV **Magnificently attired and posed in a masterly stance, HENRY VIII (1509-47) is displayed in Holbein's painting at the height of his power over Church and State**

by the Crown to willing purchasers among the 'New Men' of the century. Thus came into being a new class of landed gentry, with solid reasons for supporting the reformed religion and the Tudor dynasty. This profound change was not carried through without much turmoil and some bloodshed. The old faith and the old order had their martyrs. But the King's desires, combined with the questing temper of the age, brought about a revolution in English ways of life and habits of thought that was to have widespread effects for centuries to come.

Edward VI and Queen Mary

During the last days of December 1546, King Henry VIII died, with stoical resolution, at the age of fifty-five. He was succeeded by his only son, the offspring of Jane Seymour, born in 1537, who as Edward VI showed promise of becoming a pious and intelligent, though bigoted and strong-willed, ruler. Under the guidance of his uncle, the Protector Somerset, his royal government continued to further the progress of the English Reformation. But some of their work was temporarily undone when Edward died in 1553, and Henry's elder daughter, the child of Catherine of Aragon, a fervent supporter of the old religion, stepped into her brother's place.

Mary's unhappy existence was dominated by twin passions—her devotion to the faith that she hoped to restore, and her affection for the cold, dedicated foreign prince, later Philip II of Spain, whom she married, according to the rites of the Catholic Church, in the year that followed her enthronement. Neither passion brought her peace and happiness. Philip was frequently absent from England, attending to his dynastic duties abroad; while the task of restoring the Catholic form of worship drove her to adopt a fiercely repressive policy. After the Catholic martyrs of her father's reign came the celebrated procession of 'Marian martyrs'—obstinate Protestant enthusiasts whom the Queen's judiciary condemned to be burned to death. With her half-sister, the Princess Elizabeth, Mary's relations were suspicious and uneasy; and, after an abortive revolt led by Sir Thomas Wyatt, Elizabeth was for some months committed to the Tower of London. Then, in November 1558, the ailing Queen relinquished her grasp on life. Philip was absent; Mary collapsed and died amid the ruins of her hopes and plans. On Sunday, January 16, 1559, the twenty-five-year-old Elizabeth rode from Whitehall to be crowned Queen. 'Her Grace, by holding up her hands and merry countenance to such as stood far off, and most tender and gentle countenance to those that stood nigh . . . did declare herself no less thankfully to receive her people's good will, than they lovingly offered it unto her.' The crowds, we are told, were 'wonderfully ravished' by the demeanour of their new sovereign.

COUNTRY LIFE

97 The short reign of the sickly young king, EDWARD VI (1547-53), was dominated by Protestant influences and ended in a conspiracy to exclude his Catholic half-sister from the throne. Portrait by Holbein

98 From his 'role as Protector of the realm, the high-minded EDWARD SEYMOUR, Duke of Somerset (1506-52), was displaced by the manoeuvres of more grasping politicians

99 Acclaimed as their rightful sovereign in 1553, Mary Tudor (1553-58) estranged her subjects by her marriage to Philip II of Spain and her persecution of Protestants. MARY I AND PHILIP by Hans Eworth

Great Buildings

100   To design the **TOMB OF HENRY VII** and his consort, the Italian artist Torrigiano, who had modelled the King's bust, was again called in. The Italianate monument he produced is watched over by graceful bronze cherubs

101   Described as 'one of the most perfect buildings ever erected in England', with its exquisite fan-vaulting conceived and carried out by the Vertue brothers, **HENRY VII's CHAPEL** at Westminster Abbey was begun in 1503

102 The great cardinal diplomatist, THOMAS WOLSEY (1472-1530), directed foreign and domestic policy under Henry VIII, and governed as Lord Chancellor of England from 1515 to 1529

103 HAMPTON COURT, with its massive clock tower, was one of the splendid residences built by Wolsey for himself. After many years of increasing power and wealth, he lost his master's favour. He was disgraced, stripped of his offices and died a year later; his palace passed to the King

104 **Author, statesman and saintly humanist, SIR THOMAS MORE (1478-1535), here portrayed by Holbein seated among his family, fell a victim to Henry's royal resentment when he refused to countenance the break with Rome**

Holbein's sitters

105 **Of all Holbein's sitters, THOMAS, LORD VAUX is one of the most commanding, with his hard, resolute, masculine face confronting the perils of a hard and dangerous age**

106 **Almost as grim as the faces of his courtiers are those of Henry VIII's clerics. This is Holbein's impression of WILLIAM WARHAM (1450?-1532), Archbishop of Canterbury and political foe to Cardinal Wolsey**

107 *(below)* **In his youth, Henry was deeply devoted to every form of physical exercise. This is Holbein's arresting portrait of ROBERT CHESEMAN, the King's falconer**

108 **Despite the change of religious allegiance, many notable families remained faithful to Rome. Among them was that of THOMAS HOWARD, 3rd DUKE OF NORFOLK (1473-1554), warrior, politician and father of the poet, Surrey. Portrait by Holbein**

The Reformation

111 (*above*) **The King had no abler or more ruthless servant than THOMAS CROMWELL, later Earl of Essex (1485?-1540), who pushed on the work of the Reformation after the Act of Supremacy in 1535**

109 **Among the noblest monastic buildings pillaged by the King's Commissioners was FOUNTAINS ABBEY, a splendid Cistercian foundation established since the twelfth century**

110 (*below*) **From the ruins of the medieval abbey, a Tudor landowner built FOUNTAINS HALL. Simultaneously, many other landowners were enlarging their estates and growing rich and powerful upon the plunder of the Church**

112 **Similarly, the King relied on THOMAS CRANMER (1489-1556), the Archbishop of Canterbury who declared his union with Katherine of Aragon null, and his second marriage to Anne Boleyn valid**

113 **CRANMER'S EXECUTION AT OXFORD** followed the accession of the fiercely Catholic Mary. Convicted of heresy and condemned to be burned to death, he thrust first into the flames the hand that had signed his temporary recantation

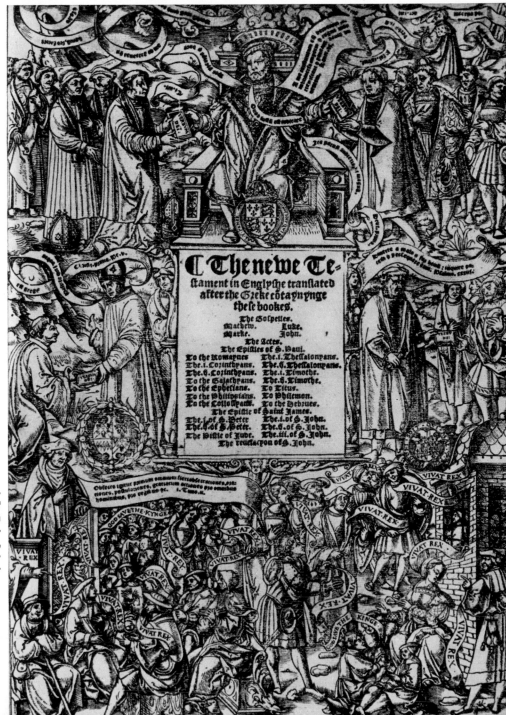

114 Under Cranmer's influence, an English translation of the Bible had been installed in churches throughout the country: **THE GREAT BIBLE,** which is also called 'Cranmer's Bible', with Henry enthroned upon the title-page

V
THE
AGE
OF
ELIZABETH

115 During her Catholic sister's reign, the young PRINCESS ELIZABETH played a perilous role, carefully avoiding involvement in conspiracy against the Crown, while watchfully biding her time

The Queen and her Servants

116 Many contemporaries thought the Queen would marry her handsome and dashing favourite, Robert Dudley, EARL OF LEICESTER (1532-88), whose long personal friendship with her gave rise to whispers of scandal

Few sovereigns have ruled with greater authority—or left a more enduring mark upon the life of a people—than Elizabeth I of England, daughter of Henry VIII and Anne Boleyn, who was born in 1533 and reigned from 1558 to 1603. At home and abroad, she impressed her contemporaries as a monarch of heroic stature; and she herself, whenever an occasion offered, gladly adopted the heroic role. This she did with consummate artistry: witness her famous oration, delivered, not long before her death, to the Speaker of the House of Commons:

'Mr Speaker, we perceive your coming is to present thanks to us. Know I accept them with . . . joy . . . Though God hath raised me high, yet this I account the glory of my crown, that I have reigned with your loves. . . . It is not my desire to live or reign longer than my life and reign shall be for your good. . . . You have had, and may have, many mightier and wiser princes sitting in this seat, yet you never had, nor shall have, any that will love you better.'

The Elizabethan House of Commons was often an unruly and recalcitrant body; but so moved were its members by the Queen's declaration of the love she bore them—and bore her other loyal subjects—that one

Plate V (*opposite*) 'I thank God,' said the Queen, 'I am endued with such qualities that if I were turned out of the realm in my petticoat, I were able to live in any place in Christendom.' It was, indeed, her combination of gifts that enabled her to dominate a brilliant age, secure in the devotion of her people. A Coronation portrait of QUEEN ELIZABETH I (1558-1603)

of them declared that it should be written in gold, and it came to be remembered as Elizabeth's 'Golden Speech'.

Yet, despite her wit, her courage and her learning, her 'fluent eloquence and princely boldness', Queen Elizabeth's direction of affairs usually showed her in a much less heroic mood. She preferred diplomacy to a show of force; rather than run unnecessary risks, she was always anxious to procrastinate and temporize; and in her relations with foreign governments she habitually played a waiting game. Many powerful forces were bent on destroying her; but, so long as she could, she held off the moment of conflict. Mary Queen of Scots—her cousin, rival and probable successor unless she could be persuaded to marry, who, expelled by her own subjects, had taken refuge with Elizabeth in the year 1568—soon became the figure-head of a secret Catholic opposition and the focus of unending plots that threatened her kinswoman's throne and life. But not until 1587 would Elizabeth agree to take decisive steps. Then she agreed only with the utmost reluctance, afterwards asserting that Mary's execution had been carried out against her will.

Similarly, she held the Spanish threat at bay by a long series of devious and guileful manoeuvres: and a peace treaty was still under consideration when the 'Invincible Armada'—spearhead of Philip II's projected conquest of England—prepared to set sail from a Spanish port. But, once the danger had materialized, Elizabeth displayed her father's spirit. 'Full of princely resolution', she rode through her forces

117 **The passionate and misguided MARY STUART, QUEEN OF SCOTS** (1542-87) who fled from her own kingdom, passed nineteen years in English custody, and was executed when the Spanish Armada threatened Elizabeth's throne. A portrait after J. Clouet

118 (*right*) **Widowed at the age of eighteen by the early death of Francis II of France, Mary returned to Scotland and married her cousin Henry Stuart, Earl of Darnley, father of the future James VI. Portrait of DARNLEY AND HIS BROTHER by Hans Eworth**

119 **Mary's third husband, James Hepburn, t**[he] adventurous **EARL OF BOTHWELL** (1536-7[8]) played a leading part in the murder of his predece[s]sor, Darnley. His charms bewitched the Queen, b[ut] not her countrymen, and his vaulting ambiti[on] contributed to her downfall

at Tilbury, 'like some Amazonian empress.' Again her gift of eloquence was seen at its best:

'Let tyrants fear!' she exclaimed. 'I have always so behaved myself that, under God, I have placed my chiefest strength and safeguard in the loyal hearts and good will of my subjects. . . . I know I have the body of a weak and feeble woman, but I have the heart and stomach of a king, and of a king of England too, and think foul scorn that . . . any prince of Europe should dare to invade the borders of my realm.'

This was on August 8, 1588. By that time, however, although there was still a danger of invasion from the Netherlands, the huge crescent-shaped squadron of Spanish ships had already been worsted in the English Channel. No sooner, battered and dispersed, had it begun its disastrous homeward voyage, than Elizabeth, whose parsimony equalled her caution, set about disbanding her troops and demobilizing her gallant but expensive fleet.

A master of state-craft herself, throughout her reign she was extraordinarily well served. Her favourites—the brilliant young men she loved to attract, Leicester, Essex, Raleigh—might be extravagant and hot-headed, but she had sober, judicious, industrious counsellors in Cecil, Walsingham and Christopher Hatton. William Cecil, her middle-class minister, afterwards ennobled as Lord Burghley, served her faithfully for forty years, until his death in 1598; and he was succeeded by his son, Robert Cecil, better known as the first Lord Salisbury. To William Cecil and his kind, aided—though sometimes impeded—by

121 The Lord High Admiral at the time of the Spanish Armada, under whom Drake and other great seamen served, was Charles, LORD HOWARD OF EFFINGHAM (1536-1624). 'We pluck their feathers little by little,' he said. A miniature by Hilliard

120 'I know I have the body of a weak and feeble woman, but I have the heart and stomach of a king, and of a king of England, too.' Thus the Queen addressed her army while the Armada was off her coasts. A portrait of ELIZABETH I by Marc Gheeraerts

The Armada

122 One hundred and thirty ships sailed from Lisbon in May 1688, carrying twenty thousand troops, who were to link with the Spanish forces in the Netherlands and over-whelm England. The ARMADA seen off Fowey, Cornwall, pursued by the English fleet. After a near-contemporary tapestry

65

their imperious, obstinate, crafty sovereign, we owe the emergence of Elizabethan England from the disorders of the Reformation period.

Builders, Explorers, Poets   Outwardly, the spirit of the age found expression in the splendid buildings it produced. The Elizabethans were ambitious builders, and while, all over England, minor gentlemen and well-to-do yeomen raised their solid manor houses—constructed according to the materials at hand, either of brick, timber and tile, or of slate or local stone—rich noblemen built themselves mansions that were known as the 'prodigy houses' of the age, vast constructions surrounding spacious courtyards, encompassed by formal gardens and extensive wooden parks. Behind the frontage—which, as at Hardwick, thanks to a multiplicity of large windows often displayed more glass than stone—in addition to withdrawing-rooms and dining-rooms there always stretched a long gallery, where, between panelled or tapestried walls, beneath a fretted plaster roof, the owner, his family and dependants could walk or converse if the weather was cold or damp. The Elizabethans appreciated luxury; but they had not yet begun to value privacy; and the rich man, as in the Middle Ages, still lived a largely public life. From birth to death, he can seldom have been alone: not until the beginning of the eighteenth century did Englishmen feel the charm of solitude. The typical Elizabethan was ostentatious, gregarious, talkative and fun-loving. He had some of the characteristics of the ancient Athenians, perpetually desirous of being told 'some new thing'.

Elizabeth's subjects were interested in the past—they devoured North's translation of Plutarch and the picturesque English chronicles composed by Hall and Holinshed; at the same time they were passionately concerned with the discoveries of the present day. Frobisher explored the north-west passage; John Hawkins and Francis Drake led expeditions through the Spanish Main; and Raleigh's attempts to found a colony in the New World helped to turn men's eyes westward. Most of these adventurers combined patriotic with commercial and

123 **Much of Queen Elizabeth's life was spent in travels about the country between her palaces and the great houses of her nobles. Here she arrives at NONSUCH, an elaborate resplendent building, constructed by her father in Surrey. From a drawing of 1562**

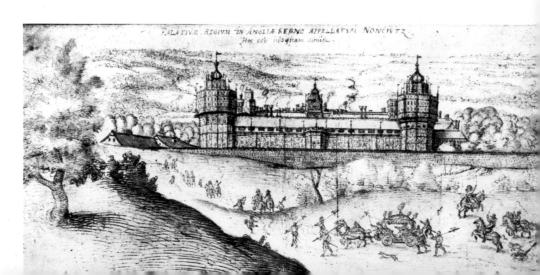

124 (*left*) Venery was pre-eminently a royal sport. The Queen feasts with her courtiers at a well-furnished HUNTING PICNIC. A woodcut from George Turbeville's 'Book of Hunting', first published in 1572

125 (*right*) The favourite of the Queen's later years, Robert Devereux, EARL OF ESSEX (1566-1601), a gallant soldier and patron of letters, who was executed after a rash and ill-organized conspiracy to remove her cautious counsellors. An engraving by Robert Boissard

piratical motives. Financing a voyage to the New World was a favourite form of enterprise among Elizabethan businessmen. Such investments were often richly rewarded. When, in the autumn of 1530, Drake sailed home on the *Golden Hind* from his triumphant circumnavigation of the globe, shareholders, who included the Queen herself, received a dividend of 4,700 per cent.

Splendour was a keynote of the age; and, notwithstanding her natural parsimony, Elizabeth kept a splendid court. Its magnificence astonished foreign diplomatists, as did the Queen's learning and wit and her fluent command of European tongues. They also commented on her love of music and dancing. But then Elizabeth's tastes were typical of the Elizabethan age, which, although acquisitive and self-seeking, was deeply devoted to the pleasures of the spirit. No major English poet had arisen since the death of Chaucer. Now, during the latter decades of the century, poets of genius began to crowd the stage. Christopher Marlowe's *Tamburlaine* was written and performed about 1587; Shakespeare, the son of a Warwickshire tradesman, reached London about 1588, and four years later was generally recognized as one of the leading playwrights of the time. Today Shakespeare may seem to stand alone; but he had numerous highly gifted rivals. The defeat of the Armada in 1588 had released a torrent of poetic activity. Englishmen, intensely proud of their heritage, were at last discovering their native genius. Just as Drake had circumnavigated the globe and returned home laden with exotic treasures, so the poets and poetic dramatists set forth to explore the territories of the mind.

The Cecils

126 **For forty years the principal minister of the Crown, cautious, painstaking but decisive, WILLIAM CECIL, LORD BURGHLEY** (1520-98), **was adept at gauging the mutable temper of the sovereign whom he faithfully served until his death**

127 **A son equal to his father in ability and power, ROBERT CECIL, EARL OF SALISBURY** (1563-1612), Secretary of State to Elizabeth I and chief minister under James I, whose peaceful accession he arranged in 1603

128 Public men vied with one another in constructing great houses fit to receive the Queen. **BURGHLEY HOUSE**, Northamptonshire, was one of two mansions built by William Cecil out of the fortune he accumulated in the service of the State

COUNTRY LIFE

Stern men in an adventurous age

131 A joint secretary of state, SIR FRANCIS WALSINGHAM (1530?-90) was the organizer of the Elizabethan secret service and one of the Puritans' chief sympathizers at Court

132 (*below*) Banker, merchant and diplomatic envoy, SIR THOMAS GRESHAM (1519-79) founded the Royal Exchange in London and gave his name to Gresham's Law, by which 'bad money drives out good'

130 The consolidator of the Church of England, JOHN WHITGIFT (1530?-1604), Archbishop of Canterbury from 1583, who in the cause of uniformity was a stern legislator against the Puritan sects

29 (*left*) When asked how he contrived to hold ministerial office throughout three very diverse reigns, William Paulet, MARQUESS OF WINCHESTER (1485-1572), is said to have replied: By being a willow, not an oak'

Dress and Manners

133 *(right)* **Children began their education early. A young nobleman, such as FRANCIS, EARL OF BEDFORD, was carefully brought up to be both courtier and scholar**

134 **SIXTEENTH-CENTURY FASHIONS** —large ruffs, padded trunk-hose and expansive farthingales—were usually showy and sumptuous rather than practical or elegant

135 *(above)* **FARMERS' WIVES, FLOWER-SELLERS AND GENTLEWOMEN** of the year 1598 display the modes of the time as they were adapted by different social classes. Elizabethan satirists inveighed against the extravagance of the age

137 *(top)* **The ELIZABETHAN TAVERN** played the same part in London life as the coffee house during the age of Anne

138 *(bottom)* **Places of amusement and dissipation were usually situated beyond the City's limits. This contemporary woodcut represents a festive GAMBLING PARTY IN A BROTHEL**

Plate VI *(opposite)* **While the art of literature flourished, contemporary painting lagged behind; and only one graphic artist of real distinction appeared in Elizabethan England —Nicholas Hilliard (1537-1619), an exquisite miniaturist, court painter to Elizabeth and James, whose fine portrait of GEORGE CLIFFORD, EARL OF CUMBERLAND was executed in 1590**

136 **Among her numerous attendants when the Queen showed herself to her subjects in her yearly progresses, was this richly liveried YEOMAN OF THE GUARD**

The first great houses

139   **Rich farmers and the lesser gentry were raising solid manor houses. A good example of these less ambitious structures is a pleasant stone-built house at TRERICE, CORNWALL**

140   **On a more grandiose scale is MONTACUT in the West country, built for a local landowne between 1588 and 1601. Like most large Elizabetha houses, it is surrounded by a formal garden**

141   **HARDWICK HALL reflects the Elizabethans' taste for splendour. With its vast extent of windows, it arose about 1594 at the command of the celebrated matriarch 'Bess of Hardwick'**

142   **The sixteenth century also left its mark on th collegiate architecture of Oxford and Cambridge QUEEN'S COLLEGE, CAMBRIDGE is a largely Tudor fabric. Here Sir Thomas More's frien Erasmus had once lived and studied**

143   *(opposite)* **The hall remained an importan feature of the English house, though many mor private rooms had now been added. The spaciou BANQUETING HALL AT KNOLE, in Kent, com bines loftiness with stately proportions**

144 **THE ARK ROYAL,** flagship of Queen Elizabeth's renowed navy. After the defeat of the Spanish Armada, it was said by a foreign observer that the English 'had become lords and masters of the sea, and need care for no man'

Adventure overseas

145 In an age of many-sided achievement, **SIR WALTER RALEIGH** (1552?-1618), here portrayed with his son, was conspicuous for the varied parts he played—as courtier, soldier, explorer, poet, sceptical philosopher and historical writer

146 **SIR RICHARD GRENVILLE** (1542-91), cousin to Raleigh, commanded the fleet that carried the first colonists to Roanoke Island, Virginia, in 1585. He died, as captain of the 'Revenge', fighting single-handed against fifteen Spanish warships

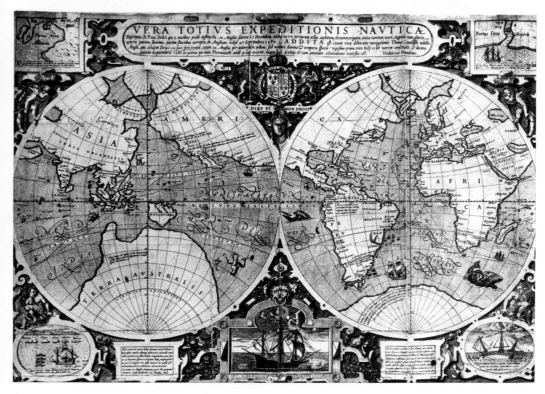

147 *(above)* **In the autumn of 1580, Drake completed his triumphant circumnavigation of the world in his ship 'Golden Hind'. Among the shareholders who reaped the rewards of this enormously profitable expedition was Queen Elizabeth herself. MAP OF DRAKE'S VOYAGES**

148 *(below)* **SIR FRANCIS DRAKE (1540?-96), nicknamed 'the Dragon' by his Spanish adversaries, began to attack Spanish shipping and pillage the treasures of the New World while the sovereigns of England and Spain were still nominally at peace**

149 **CHARLES BLOUNT, LORD MOUNTJOY (1563-1606), Lord Deputy of Ireland, and a successful general in Elizabeth's Irish wars. A close associate of her unruly favourite, the Earl of Essex, whose rebellious designs he had at first encouraged**

Gloriana and her poets

151   Poet and romantic novelist, author of the
pastoral narrative 'Arcadia', which he wrote to
entertain his beloved sister Lady Pembroke, SIR
PHILIP SIDNEY (1554-86) epitomized for the
Eizabethans their conception of dashing chivalric
youth

150   Describing THE QUEEN IN HER LAST YEARS, a
foreign ambassador wrote admiringly of her 'fine and
vigorous disposition'. But her teeth were blackened, and her
face was 'long and thin and very aged', topped with a great
auburn wig. Unfinished miniature by Hilliard

152 More erudite than Shakespeare, whose
rapid ascent he seems to have regarded with some
surprise and consternation, BEN JONSON
(1572-1637) was an accomplished lyricist and one
of the massive pillars of the Elizabethan stage

153 (*below*) The multiform genius of WILLIAM
SHAKESPEARE (1564-1616) first showed signs
of emerging five years after the defeat of the
Armada. With the modest fortune his talents had
earned him, he retired to Stratford about 1610

154 Lyrical, historical, topographical,
the literary undertakings of MICHAEL
DRAYTON (1563-1631) covered a remarkably wide field. But he is best remembered as the author of one of the
loveliest sonnets in the English language

VI

KING AND PARLIAMENT

156 Described by Henri IV of France as 'the wisest fool in Christendom', Elizabeth's ungainly successor JAMES I OF ENGLAND AND VI OF SCOTLAND (1603-1625) was probably the most erudite monarch who has ever occupied the throne

An age of Enquiry

155 An extraordinarily gifted philosophical writer, who early in life announced that he had 'taken all knowledge to be his province', FRANCIS BACON (1561-1626) was also an ambitious and, at times, an unscrupulous politician

When King James VI of Scotland crossed the frontier at Berwick-upon-Tweed on April 6, 1603, he was welcomed with rejoicing by his new English subjects. To him, and to the Scottish courtiers who accompanied him on his leisurely journey to London, England seemed a land of plenty in which they would now happily share. And indeed, during most of the four decades that followed there was much that was glittering, hopeful and admirable upon the English scene. The first forty years of the seventeenth century saw performed many of Shakespeare's greatest plays, and those of his more romantic and tortuous younger contemporaries; they witnessed the elaboration of courtly entertainment in the masque, with its spectacular blending of music, verse, dancing, costume and scenery; they were adorned by the splendid Palladian buildings of Inigo Jones, who brought an exquisitely proportioned new style from Italy to England and began to enshrine it in the palace of Whitehall and elsewhere. An age rich in elegant lyric poets, it was also distinguished by the stirrings of the spirit of philosophical and scientific enquiry evident in the works of Bacon. Its divines and men of learning expressed themselves in some of the finest and most eloquent prose that has ever been written in the language. They composed the famous translation of the Bible under the personal authority of King James, whose most enduring monument it remains.

This was not an age of martial glory or of national prowess on the world's political stage. All King James's and King Charles's European

Plate VII (*opposite*) Despite flattering official portraits, CHARLES I (1625-49) had, like his father James, a short and unimpressive figure. Unlike James, he was notably dignified, led a virtuous domestic life, and had a high sense of moral obligation; though, as a ruler, he sometimes mistook double-dealing for diplomacy. After a portrait by Mytens

Robert Winter   Christopher Wrigt   Iohn Wrigt   Thomas Percy   Guido Fawkes   Robert Catefby   Th Wi

157 **Infuriated by the increasing severity of anti-Catholic legislation, a group of English Catholic gentlemen, including an ex-soldier named Guy Fawkes, planned to blow up, on November 5, 1605, the King and all his faithful Commons. But an anonymous letter revealed the GUNPOWDER PLOT, and Fawkes paid the penalty**

adventures failed. But it was a period of remarkable intellectual, literary and religious endeavour, and of developing colonial and commercial adventure. One achievement of the times looms very large to later eyes, although when it took place it must have seemed an unpredictable by-product of prevailing zeal and enterprise. This was the foundation of the first American colonies, a small beginning and lodgment that was to have momentous consequences in the new continent and, in the course of time, for the world.

The Political Scene

Meanwhile, in the British Isles and especially in England, beneath the surface of old customs and new accomplishments, forces were at work that presently plunged the country into bitter civil war and startling revolution. Parliament, in the last years of Elizabeth I, had met in awe of the Virgin Queen who had saved the realm, but it was nevertheless increasingly assertive of its rights and ready to doubt the wisdom of government. Under her successors, the Stuarts, Parliament's claims steadily grew to the point where it demanded to debate the decisions of government and even to share in making them. The new classes of country gentry and substantial burgesses, along with some of the recently ennobled families, who all owed their status to the Reformation and the pace of commercial advance, were pressing for a say in the exercise of power.

King James, and his son after him for so long as he could, maintained the divine right of kings to rule as they pleased, and conservatively resisted all inroads on their prerogative. Their Parliaments were at first equally conservative in the political grounds they put forward. They based themselves on medieval precedents, now interpreted in a light formidable to the royal position, and only gradually moved into a revolutionary stance. The royal position was in itself weaker than in Tudor times. The country still expected the king to meet the ordinary costs of government out of his traditional resources, Parliament making extraordinary grants of taxation only for emergencies such as war. But prices had been steadily rising, during a century of inflation, and with them the costs of government went up. Nor were matters mended by the optimistic extravagance of the early Stuarts' courts. This growing financial problem rapidly led to disputes over the King's right to levy special taxation. For a time, the Stuarts tided over affairs by reviving medieval taxes, granting monopolies for sums in cash, selling honours and using every money-raising expedient at hand. But a clash could not be forever postponed between the principles of the king's rights in government and of accountability to his peoples. It came when King Charles I, on a wrong policy, and for the highest motives, plunged into difficulties with his Scottish and Irish kingdoms. His embarrassments were then Parliament's opportunity.

159 **Against the rising tide of Puritan agitation, WILLIAM LAUD (1573-1645), Archbishop of Canterbury, strenuously supported the Established Church. Three years after the outbreak of the Civil War, he was condemned to mount the scaffold. Portrait by Mytens**

The Puritan Strain

Mingled with the political and financial difficulties of the age, and exacerbating them, were religious divisions, multiplying and weighing heavily upon earnest consciences, and soon to play a principal part in the outbreak and conduct of civil war. Under the Elizabethan settlement early in the Queen's reign, the Church of England had been re-established on a broad basis, intended to appeal to the great majority of national Protestant opinion. The second half of the sixteenth-century, however, had seen the triumph of Presbyterianism in the Church of Scotland and its dissemination in England, together with other doctrines and observances in religion, more and less extremist, commonly described as Puritan. As the Puritan party grew in strength under the first two Stuarts, some of its leaders found it natural to proceed from the plea for liberty of conscience in private belief to a demand for unprecedented liberties of the subject in public affairs. A radical faith in religion began to be accompanied by radical views in politics, and Puritanism and the Parliamentary opposition found themselves allies in action. In the meantime, the Church of England, under the impetus of Charles I's close adviser, Archbishop Laud, became an increasingly severe critic and persecutor of Puritanism. In its rites and usages the English Church seemed to many god-fearing people to be dangerously approaching a Roman Catholic outlook. The radical Protestants were thereby the more provoked, and, for the first time since Queen Elizabeth's accession, loyalty to the Crown and belief in the many forms of the Protestant faith ceased to be synonymous.

These problems had simmered under the lax, peaceful, corrupt reign of James I; under his son's they burst into flame. In contrast to the shambling, pedantic and coarse-grained personality of King James, Charles was a dignified figure, most upright in morals, gifted with a fine discerning taste, and with lofty intentions. He is best known to us from the elegant portraits by his court painter, Vandyck, who was remarkably successful at concealing his sitter's smallness of stature. Proudly convinced of the virtues of his own royal station, King Charles had the misfortune to consider double-dealing permissible in a monarch. A curiously vacillating character, now buoyantly firm, now in appearance ready to make any concession, he found himself led, through a natural want of political sensitiveness, deeper and deeper into an impossible constitutional situation from which only a trial at arms could result.

The Civil War

Early in his reign King Charles had received a sharp shock from Parliament. Engaged in a fruitless campaign against France, he had been obliged to summon a Parliament in order to ask for finance, and Parliament had retaliated with a concise statement of its electors' grievances. The French war came to an inconclusive end, and Parliament was dissolved; but the grievances remained and festered during the ten following years of personal rule by the King. They burst forth vehemently when strife broke out with the Scots, on whom Charles and Archbishop Laud were attempting to impose a High-Church establishment, alien to the traditions of the Kirk. Once more Parliaments were summoned—a short one, which broke up in anger, and then the celebrated Long Parliament, the instrument of the English Revolution, which first met on November 3, 1640.

This Parliament, under the leadership of John Pym, launched its attack upon the King's chief minister, Thomas Wentworth, Earl of Strafford, whom it considered to be the would-be architect of absolutism. Strafford was brought to trial and, in spite of the King's efforts to save him, condemned for treason and executed. Archbishop Laud was also arrested and later put to death. Thus were the King's ministers arraigned, while his policies lay in ruins. Parliament now inaugurated an extensive series of reforms, designed to prevent the recurrence of a period of personal rule by the sovereign. Its radical and Puritan ambitions were aided from an unlikely quarter. At this moment, the oppressed Catholic masses of Ireland broke into revolt against their landowners, against Protestantism and against English rule. Parliament in London seized the chance to raise its claims; it sought to

160 A faithful servant to his royal master, 'Black Tom Tyrant' to his foes, THOMAS WENTWORTH, EARL OF STRAFFORD (1593-1641) was sacrificed by the King on the insistence of the House of Commons

161   To his vivacious and headstrong French consort, the King proved a devoted husband. Vandyck's portrait of the **CHILDREN OF CHARLES I** shows two future sovereigns, Charles II and James II, as well as Henrietta or 'Minette', Charles II's beloved sister, who married the brother of Louis XIV

nominate the commanders of any royal army sent to suppress the Irish rebellion; further, it demanded that henceforth the King should only employ Ministers approved by Parliament. Not for the last time, an Irish initiative deflected the course of English politics. For this was the turning point from which modern Parliamentary government in England really dates its origins. It was also the point at which civil war became inevitable. The King would not accept Parliament's views, and he thought, with some justice, that he had much backing in the country for his resistance to the Parliamentary revolt.

In the eyes of many moderates, Parliament had gone too far. In fact, more than a third of the Members of the House of Commons and most of the peers supported the King. They ceased to attend Parliament in London, which gradually by successive defections and purges dwindled into a small assembly, to be derisively known as the 'Rump'. When the King decided to put matters to the test, and raised his standard at Nottingham in August 1642, he felt he had at least half the country with him, and the fiercely fought battles of the next three years proved him right. The country was clearly split into two, although no single description of the dividing line could be accurate. Only in part was it a matter of Royalist versus Parliamentarian, High Churchman versus Puritan, old gentry versus new wealth, North and West versus South and East. Loyalties and the principles criss-crossed with a complexity

162 (*opposite*) The uncompromising Catholicism of **QUEEN HENRIETTA MARIA** (1609-66) aroused much resentment in her new country. She lived to see her husband executed and, eventually, her eldest son restored to power

163 and 164 **At one o'clock on the cold afternoon of January 30, 1649, Charles I —henceforward 'KING CHARLES THE MARTYR' in the mind of every English royalist—stepped from a first-floor window of Inigo Jones' BANQUETING HOUSE, across a scaffold built above Whitehall, to meet death with his accustomed dignity. Before he lay down, he helped the executioner to arrange a small white satin cap. When his head was shown to the crowd, 'there was such a groan by the thousands there present' as a contemporary writer hoped that he might never hear again**

that gave rise to an enormous contemporary literature, and members of the same family served on opposite sides.

The King in the end lost the struggle. By 1645 his forces were everywhere beaten. After an uneasy peace, in which he tried to play off his enemies one against the other, Charles stepped to his execution on January 30, 1649, upon a scaffold erected outside his own Banqueting House in Whitehall. It was not, however, Parliament that had effectively triumphed, but the Parliamentary generals, and one in particular—Oliver Cromwell.

Oliver Cromwell

A rustic gentleman, and at first an inconspicuous Member of Parliament, with no military experience until his forty-fourth year, Cromwell rose to eminence, and then to supreme power, through genius in war. If he was only one of several able Parliamentary commanders to whom Charles owed his defeat, he alone was the leader and organizer of victory in Ireland, in Scotland, against Charles II at Worcester and in campaigns overseas. First as the Lord General of the Commonwealth and then as Lord Protector, Cromwell's will was for ten years the

165 **A country gentleman and Member of Parliament who only in middle age became a formidable commander in arms, OLIVER CROMWELL (1599-1658) found Britain at his feet when the Civil War ended; first as Lord General and then as Lord Protector, he made his will the nation's will. Portrait by S. Cooper**

nation's will. Sustained by a compact veteran army, he exercised over a Puritan Republic an authority that few English kings had wielded even in medieval times. Residing in the former royal palaces of Whitehall and Hampton Court, he maintained a show of state worthy of his position. In public business his capacious mind and robust strength of personality were equal to every challenge at home and abroad, save one. Anxious debates in the Commonwealth and Protectorate, which abounded in democratic ideas, hardly heard of again until the French Revolution, and several earnestly intended experiments in representation at Westminster, failed to solve the constitutional problem of reconciling Parliamentary principle with executive power. Cromwell sought to legalize and perpetuate his régime, but never found a way of doing so. During his last years, his government was in effect a military dictatorship conducted by eleven major-generals under his command. It was firm, successful and in the eyes of its sympathizers glorious. But it rested on a personal foundation, and when the Great Protector died on September 3, 1658, the imposing edifice he had built ignobly collapsed about the heads of his successors.

Two reigns

166 **JAMES I AS A BOY was brought up in a harsh and exacting school—disputed over, threatened, humiliated by the greedy and factious Scottish nobles. His experiences left a permanent scar**

168 (*below*) **In the reign of Elizabeth a brilliant young worldling and a curiously original poet, JOHN DONNE (1573-1631) became, under James and Charles, a deeply devout and strongly eloquent divine**

167 (*above*) **Unable to forget his own physical and moral shortcomings, James was always drawn towards handsome and attractive favourites, among whom none played a more disastrous part than GEORGE VILLIERS, DUKE OF BUCKINGHAM (1592-1628)**

169 (*above*) **Most of Vandyck's official portraits of the King give us his conception of an ideal sovereign, just as elsewhere he depicted an ideal aristocracy. These preparatory STUDIES OF CHARLES I have a somewhat more realistic air**

170 (*above*) **St John's College, Oxford, founded in 1555, received a magnificent addition during the early seventeenth century—CANTERBURY QUAD-RANGLE (1631-36), with the King's statue high above the gate**

171 (*below*) **In the armies of his uncle Charles I, PRINCE RUPERT (1619-82) won distinction as a dashing cavalry commander; he is shown standing on the left with two of his colonels**

The Social Scene

172 A typical Royalist country gentleman was Sir John Byron, later first
LORD BYRON, an ancestor of the
great Romantic poet, who fought with
distinction at Edgehill and the battle of
Roundaway Down. Portrait by Dobson

173 (*above*) **To sit for her picture by Cornelius Johnson, ANNE UVEDALE, after-
wards Mrs Henslowe, disguised herself as
the Goddess Flora, with a fantastic coronal
of flowers and feathers**

174 (*right*) **The arrogance of youth and
the pride of birth are both reflected in
Vandyck's memorable representation of
the Lords JOHN AND BERNARD
STUART, wearing the extravagant court
fashions of the day**

175 One of the 'young eagles' at the court of James I was EDWARD SACK-VILLE, EARL OF DORSET, a nobleman renowned both for his gallantries and for the splendid personal state he kept

176 Said in early youth to have been Dorset's mistress, VENETIA DIGBY is here painted by Vandyck as the wife of the famous Sir Kenelm Digby, whose learning and talents made him 'The Age's Wonder' to his contemporaries

177 Probably designed with the help of Inigo Jones or one of his disciples, the west front of CASTLE ASHBY, constructed about 1630, shows the new Italianate trend in English architecture

'COUNTRY LIFE'

178 Son of the renowned scientist known as 'the Wizard Earl', ALGERNON, TENTH EARL OF NORTHUMBERLAND, held in 1638 the office of Lord High Admiral. Portrait by Vandyck

London and Parliament

180 **Champion of the opposition to arbitrary taxation, JOHN HAMPTON (1594-1643) raised a regiment to fight for the Parliamentary cause and died of wounds received in battle**

179   **Step by step Parliament passed from the voicing of grievances to claiming a share in the making of government decisions: THE TWO HOUSES, with Charles presiding over the Lords**

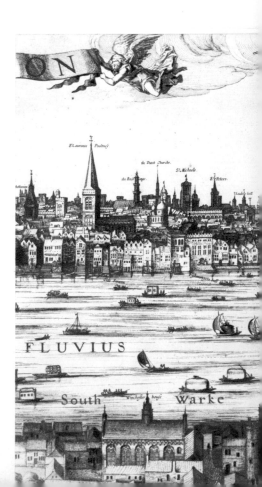

181 **The Parliamentary leader who forced the pace of the Great Rebellion, JOHN PYM (1584-1643). He died in the second year of the war, having launched a revolution that destroyed the possibility of absolute monarchy**

183 **At the lowest ebb of royalist fortunes Thomas Hobbes (1588-1679) published his political philosophy, in which he argued the case for a powerful state that would compel aggressive human nature to live in peace: title-page of THE LEVIATHAN, 1651**

182 (*left*) **The citizens of London played a notable part in the resistance to royal rule and were firm in their support of the House of Commons: a detail from Visscher's MAP OF LONDON, 1616, showing the Bridge**

Cromwell

**184 THE GREAT SEAL OF THE
LORD PROTECTOR** of the Republics
of England, Scotland and Ireland, on
which Cromwell rides against a background view of London and the Thames

**185 Trampling on 'Babylon' and 'Error', while surrounded by trophies of victory and vignettes of
peaceful progress, CROMWELL appears in an engraving of 1658 as the 'Emblem of England's
attained and further expected freedom and happiness'**

186 The most successful of Parliamentary commanders, **SIR THOMAS FAIRFAX (1612-71)**, whose conservative nature was gradually estranged by the quarrel between Army and Parliament and Cromwell's rise to supremacy. Portrait after R. Walker

190 (*above*) **Husband of Cromwell's daughter, Bridget, General CHARLES FLEETWOOD** played a vacillating part in the twilight of the Protectorate. Miniature by S. Cooper

189 (*below*) **The mid-sixteenth century saw the origin of British newspapers. MERCURIUS RUSTICUS** was one of several periodical sheets that waged the verbal campaigns of the Civil War

187 (*above*) **After Cromwell's death, the brilliant General JOHN LAMBERT (1619-83)** had hopes of inheriting his mantle but was outmanoeuvred by the restorers of Charles II. A portrait by Ferdinand Bol

188 (*below*) **Cromwell and his family kept royal state at Whitehall and Hampton Court. His ablest son HENRY CROMWELL (1628-74)** served his father in the wars and held the post of Lord Deputy of Ireland. Portrait by R. Walker

VII

THE THIRTEEN COLONIES

191 The voyages of Christopher Columbus led to strange conjectures in European minds about the wonders of America. This imaginative woodcut of **INDIAN CANNIBALS** dates from 1505, thirteen years after his first landfall in the West Indies

Elizabethan Enterprise

The British, who were to pass on their language and many of their institutions to the future United States, arrived comparatively late upon the American scene. John Cabot's expedition to Newfoundland in the reign of Henry VII had no immediate sequel; and, although by the middle of the sixteenth century, English adventurers were reaching out towards Muscovy, Africa and Brazil, North America remained untouched by their efforts. Two other European nations, however, were already penetrating into its mainland from opposite quarters of the continent. The French, based on the St Lawrence, had begun their explorations by traders and missionaries of the Great Lakes and the basin of the Mississippi; while the expeditions of the Spaniards from Mexico and the Caribbean were ranging over Florida, Louisiana and the territories that became the states of the American south-west.

English endeavours in Queen Elizabeth's reign were at first concentrated upon the search for a passage to the riches of the Indies, by way of the Canadian north-west. This series of pioneer voyages ended

192 The promoters of the Virginia company issued pamphlets in 1609, advertising to investors and settlers the 'MOST EXCELLENT FRUITS' to be gained from plantations in the new colony. The ship is of the kind in which the Jamestown migrants sailed

in frustration, and the British lodgment in Canada had to await the foundation of the Hudson's Bay Company in the days of Charles II. But gradually, and for a variety of reasons, the idea of planting permanent colonies in North America was growing and finding acceptance in England. There was the hope of profit from mines, from the fur-trade and from fishing. There was the strategic motive of securing a base on the flank of the Spanish empire that would prove its value in struggles to come. Some far-sighted promoters also recognized that colonies could provide a reinforcement to the strength of the home country, serving as an outlet for population and exports, and as a source of raw materials. The theories that later inspired the mercantile colonial system were already in the making. Mingled with these material and patriotic considerations, in a manner typical of the age, were lofty ideals of religious advancement. As the Virginia Charter put it in 1606, the purposes of the new Company should include the 'propagating of Christian religion to such people as live in darkness and miserable

193 **CAPTAIN JOHN SMITH** (1558-1631), president of the Jamestown council, explorer of Virginia and cartographer of the New England coast, became the first historian in English of the North American colonies

ignorance of the true knowledge and worship of God'. A differently accented, but not dissimilar, theme was shortly to inspire the Puritan emigration.

The Virginia Company

Virginia, named in honour of Queen Elizabeth, had been the site of two English attempts at settlement after Raleigh had sent his first scouting expedition to the American coast in 1584. Roanoke Island, off what is now North Carolina, was their base; both failed to take root, however, although one made a promising start. Thereafter, for nearly twenty years, English overseas efforts were cut short, engulfed in the war with Spain. Peace brought renewed opportunity, and the famous landing of some one hundred adventurers at Jamestown on the Chesapeake Bay took place on May 24, 1607. A long and arduous struggle under the leadership of Captain John Smith was needed before the colony's survival was certain; but here at last the American nation saw its start. In its origins, the enterprise was a corporate and commercial one, intended to yield profits to its directors in London, as the trade of the Muscovy and East India Companies was expected to do. But matters in the New World took a decisively different course. The English promoters saw few returns, and by the end of King James's reign their Company had ceased to exist. Virginia became a royal colony, and the problem began to arise of the proper relationship between Crown

Plate VIII (*opposite*) **The life and customs of the Indian tribes in Virginia stirred the imagination of Englishmen, and the occasional Indian visitor to Europe was treated with flattering curiosity. INDIANS FISHING by John White**

and Colonies that was to vex the communities on both sides of the Atlantic for the next hundred and fifty years.

At the same time, another development had taken place, of great significance for the American future. John Rolfe, the husband of Pocahontas, experimented successfully with the growing and curing of tobacco, and Virginia's fortunes soon came to be based on the cultivation of the crop. A planters' society was emerging that would distinguish the old South from its Northern neighbours. Alongside indentured labourers and craftsmen, arriving in increasing numbers from England, negroes were imported from Africa to work on the plantations. The 'peculiar institution' of the South that was to lead to the formidable struggle with the North had its origins in the purchase, in Rolfe's words, of 'twenty Negars' from a Dutch privateer in 1619.

The Pilgrim Fathers

To the north of Virginia, in the region christened New England by Captain John Smith, other English companies had for some time been vainly but hopefully attempting to found fresh centres of colonization. Achievement here was to spring not from commercial enterprise, but from the prompting of religious zeal and the demand for liberty of conscience. The Pilgrim Fathers brought with them from Europe a tradition that was to have an even profounder influence on the American way of life than that of Virginia. They came to the shores of

Ætatis suæ 21. Ã. 1616.

194   In legend the saviour of John Smith's life, POCAHONTAS, daughter of the Indian chief, Powhattan, married the colonist John Rolfe; she died in 1617 on a visit to England, where her portrait was painted in Jacobean costume

America seeking a refuge from the sins and oppressions of the old world. America was for them the land of salvation, in which a freer and more just society was to be built.

When the *Mayflower* sailed from Plymouth in September 1620, she bore thirty-five members from the English Puritan congregation that had spent thirteen years of uncomfortable exile in Holland, and sixty-six West Country pioneers of varying religious persuasion, and by no means all of high-minded disposition. The little township they founded by Plymouth Rock received a formal patent from the Crown; but in spirit it was governed from the first by the celebrated *Mayflower* compact drawn up among the Pilgrims themselves. 'Having undertaken,' they declared, 'for the glory of God, and advancement of the Christian faith, and honour of our King and country, a voyage to plant the first colony in the northern parts of Virginia, [we] do by these presents solemnly and mutually in the presence of God, and one of another, covenant and combine ourselves together into a civil body politic, for our better ordering and preservation and furtherance of the ends aforesaid; and by virtue hereof do enact, constitute, and frame such just and equal laws, ordinances, acts, constitutions, and offices, from time to time, as shall be thought most meet and convenient for the general good of the colony, unto which we promise all due submission and obedience.'

Thus William Bradford and his colleagues drew up a kind of constitu-

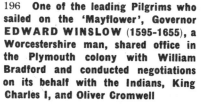

196 One of the leading Pilgrims who sailed on the 'Mayflower', Governor **EDWARD WINSLOW (1595-1655)**, a Worcestershire man, shared office in the Plymouth colony with William Bradford and conducted negotiations on its behalf with the Indians, King Charles I, and Oliver Cromwell

195 The Massachusetts Bay Colony flourished from the start. Its prime citizen from 1630 onwards was Governor **JOHN WINTHROP (1588-1649)**, a Puritan lawyer from Suffolk, England, who served twelve terms as Governor of Boston

197 **The last and almost legendary Director-General of New Netherland was PETER STUYVESANT (1592-1672), who stumped ashore on his wooden leg in 1647; he nourished a dream of New Amsterdam as the most important city of the Atlantic seaboard**

198 **Five years after the Pilgrims landed at Plymouth, the Dutch, who had already penetrated into the Hudson valley, purchased the island of Manhattan for trinkets worth twenty-four dollars. A view of the STADT HUYS in NEW YORK, engraved in 1679**

tional document, based upon the doctrine of the general good, that echoed down the generations until it received its momentous confirmation at Philadelphia in 1776.

The Eastern Springboard

Plymouth marked only a small beginning; but many New England settlements followed, most powerful among them being those of the Massachusetts Bay Company. In 1630 its Governor, John Winthrop, cleared a site at the mouth of the Charles River that was to become the City of Boston and, in time, the seat of rebellion against British rule. From Massachusetts Bay, groups of settlers steadily radiated outwards to form new townships on the Connecticut River, in Rhode Island, in New Hampshire and elsewhere, some in search of better farming lands, others in pursuit of religious freedom. Gradually the northern colonies took shape, their stern countryside and rocky shores breeding the Yankee character—the god-fearing, hard-trading, liberty-loving epitome of republican ideals.

To the south Maryland was added in the reign of Charles I to the ranks of the courtly-founded colonies, and the Carolinas were settled under his son. Between lay the Dutch on the Hudson river and the Swedes in Delaware, both to be embraced within the British orbit in

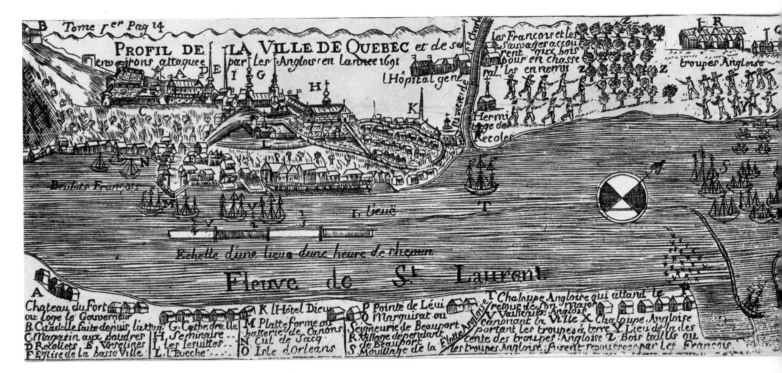

199 **The French settlement at Quebec grew slowly but steadily throughout the century, and from a trading post sprang the foundations of a city; a VIEW OF QUEBEC in 1690**

1664. Indeed, perhaps the most notably lasting result of the Anglo-Dutch struggles of the seventeenth century was the transformation of little New Amsterdam into old New York.

By the end of the century, the Jerseys had been founded and William Penn had launched his Quaker commonwealth, reinforced by the first wave of German immigration, in Philadelphia. Except for Georgia, the thirteen colonies had all been born, and most of them had found their feet. Over a quarter of a million farmers, traders, planters, fishermen and their families were scattered down the east coast of the continent from the borders of Canada to the neighbourhood of Florida, their settlements reaching inland from the ocean towards the Appalachians, beyond which lay the Indian west. Separate in their foundation and distinct in their outlook, the colonies as yet aspired to no general association among themselves. But with England, whether under Cromwell or the restored Stuarts, their relations were already beginning to be strained by the laws of navigation and trade that protected British interests, often at American expense. In the immediate future, the menace of France, from the north and west of the continent, hung heavily over the scene. Until it was finally dispelled, the fortunes of Britain and America were to remain inseparably allied.

Massachusetts

201 **A god-fearing survivor from the earlie** colonial days, ANNE POLLARD with her Bible painted in 1721 by an anonymous limner whe she was a hundred years old

200 (*left*) An outstanding leader of the Puritan theocracy in Massachusetts was **INCREASE MATHER** (1639-1723), pastor of North Church, Boston, and President of Harvard College; he was the father of the famous Puritan Minister, Cotton Mather. Portrait by Van der Spriett, 1688

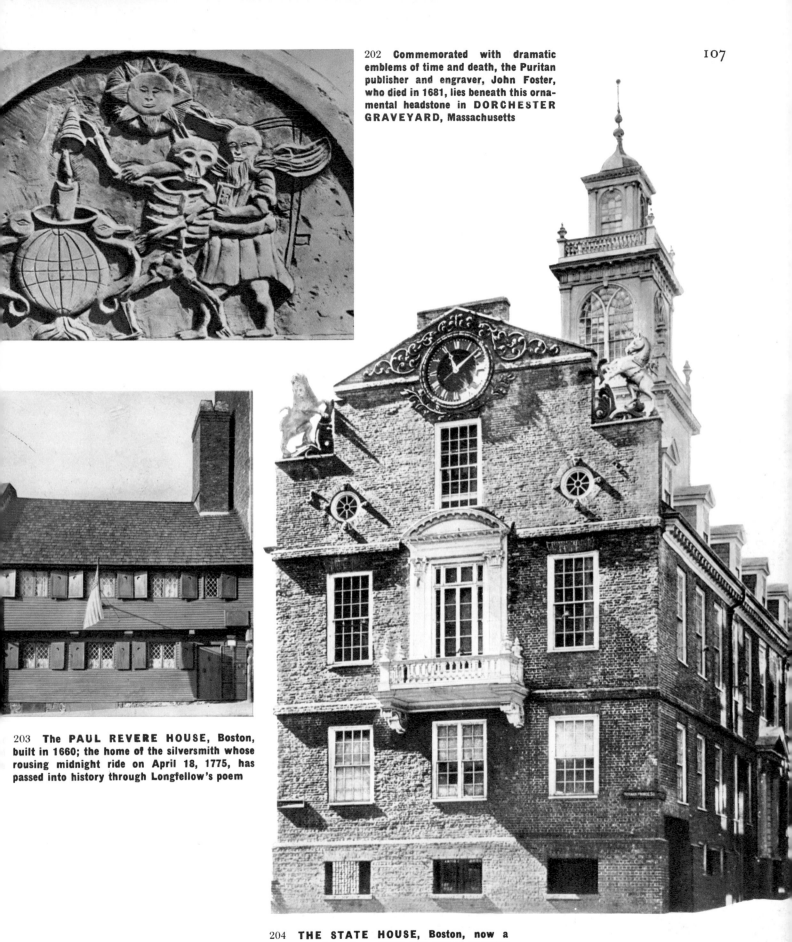

202 **Commemorated with dramatic emblems of time and death, the Puritan publisher and engraver, John Foster, who died in 1681, lies beneath this ornamental headstone in DORCHESTER GRAVEYARD, Massachusetts**

203 **The PAUL REVERE HOUSE, Boston, built in 1660; the home of the silversmith whose rousing midnight ride on April 18, 1775, has passed into history through Longfellow's poem**

204 **THE STATE HOUSE, Boston, now a museum, dates from 1713 and has a graceful dignity similar to that of contemporary Queen Anne buildings in England**

Virginia

The earliest delineations of the American scene are JOHN WHITE'S DRAWINGS OF VIRGINIA. The artist was one of the settlers landed on Roanoke in 1585 by Grenville and repatriated by Drake. He was governor of Raleigh's second colony in 1587, which disappeared during his absence. When White returned to Roanoke four years later, he found carved on a doorpost the mysterious word 'Croatoan', which has suggested that the colonists joined the Croatan Indians

205   One of the wives of Chief Wyngyno

206   Indian women sowing corn and men hoeing

207   'One of their religious men'

209   'Sitting at meate'

208   Native warriors in a circular dance

Plate IX (*opposite*) 'Apostle to the Indians', the Puritan JOHN ELIOT (1604-90), who came to Massachusetts from Hertfordshire, England, in 1631, propagated the Gospel among the neighbouring tribes, and published his famous Indian translation of the Bible

JOHN ELIOT

PREACHER to the INDIANS in NEW ENGLAND

PROGRESS
OF THE
GOSPEL
AMONGST
THE
INDIANS
IN
NEW ENGLAND

New Amsterdam...

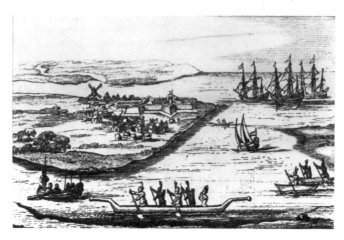

211   **The first known view of NEW AMSTERDAM, probably dating from 1626, shows the Dutch West India Company settlement as it was planned to be rather than as it was**

210   **A touch of austere elegance marks this portrait of CORNELIUS STEENWYCK, mayor of New York under British rule in 1668-69; below is an inset view of the town**

212   **Under the governorship of Peter Stuyvesant, the European population of New Netherland numbered barely fifteen hundred, of which one-third lived amid the 'boweries' of MANHATTAN: a view of the island in the mid-seventeenth century**

213 (*right*)   **In 1673 a Dutch expedition temporarily re-occupied New York; a detail, one and a half times the original size, from the RESTITUTIO map and view engraved to celebrate the event**

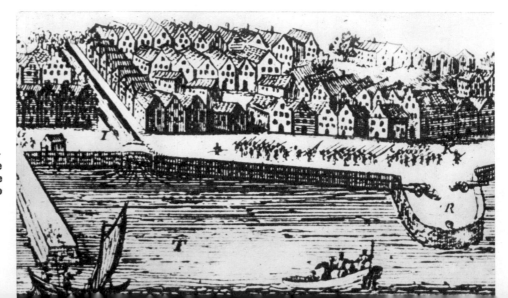

. becomes New York

214 The **NEW DUTCH CHURCH** on Nassau Street, as drawn by William Burgis in 1731; coaches, such as the one shown, were by now common among wealthy New Yorkers

215 The **BAKEWELL VIEW** of New York, dating from the early eighteenth century, reveals a city that was beginning to rival Boston and Philadelphia in size and importance

216 The descendants of the Dutch patroons, down to the days of the Presidents Theodore and Franklin Delano Roosevelt, exercised an abiding influence on the American scene: CAPTAIN AND MRS JOHANNES SCHUYLER of Albany, capital of New York State

The colonies come of age

218   **THE ARK**, one of the two ships in which Baltimore's two hundred colonists, many of them Roman Catholics, sailed to Maryland in 1634. This relief is at Hook Manor, Tisbury, Wiltshire

219   The founder of a 'holy experiment' in political and religious liberty in the state that bears his name, **WILLIAM PENN** (1644-1718) and, 220, his wife **HANNAH**. Contemporary chalk drawings by Francis Place

221 (*below*) **A contemporary view of the first settlement in SOUTH CAROLINA, 1670, near modern Charleston. An elaborate constitution was drawn up for the colony by the philosopher, John Locke, but it was never adopted by the Assembly**

217 (*opposite*) **The first proprietor of Maryland, Cecilius Calvert, LORD BALTIMORE (1605-75), received his grant from King Charles I in 1632 and governed his province through deputies, one of whom was his son. A portrait by G. Soest**

An individual people

222   Among the craftsmen who brought the art of painting to the New World was Evert Duyckink.
This LUNCHEON PARTY is attributed to one of his descendants who followed his calling

223 In the early eighteenth-century New York was rich in portraitists; the BOY WITH DEER is painted in the Dutch-inspired manner known as 'de Peyster'

224 'DEAL WITH YOUR QUAKING FRIEND'; a playing-card advertising the sale of lands in Pennsylvania

225 'TO FOOL AWAY A SPORTING SUM IN NORTH AMERICA'; a playing card satirizing colonial settiement

226 General JAMES OGLETHORPE (1696-1785) founded Georgia in 1732-33 and led the colony's forces against the Spaniards to the South. In later life Oglethorpe was an honoured member of Dr Johnson's circle in London

VIII

THE RESTORATION

227 **With agile diplomacy, backed by his command of a considerable army, General GEORGE MONCK (1608-70) secured the restoration of Charles II on the promise of a 'free Parliament' and 'liberty of tender consciences'. Miniature by Cooper**

What was restored in 1660? Certainly the monarchy, the Church of England and the bishops were re-established, but so also was the authority of Parliament. All the Acts limiting the powers of the Crown, to which Charles I had been obliged to consent before the outbreak of the civil war, remained valid and were now put back into force. Most of the powerful Army that had dominated the country under Cromwell was peaceably disbanded. The Restoration marked an end, for the time being, of political experiment and a return to constitutionalism. For the people of England had caught a glimpse of anarchy in the year that followed Cromwell's death, in which the country seemed about to fall a prey to contending Army generals. When General Monck decided to march on London and call for a free Parliament that would invite the King to return, he was responding to a national desire for stability of institutions.

King Charles II was welcomed not only by faithful royalists, but by all who wished to put a stop to the dangers of armed strife. The battles of the immediate future were to be political battles, marked by

228 Statesman, and historian of the Great Rebellion, EDWARD HYDE, EARL OF CLARENDON, (1609-74), after years of war and exile, helped to negotiate the return of the King and presided over the restored royal government. After a portrait by Gerard Soest

229 One of his courtiers remarked of CHARLES II (1660-85) that 'he never said a foolish thing, and never did a wise one', to which the King replied that his words were his own, but his actions were his Ministers. Amid the problems of the age he adroitly picked his way. Miniature by Cooper

230 Charles II's Queen, CATHERINE OF BRAGANZA (1638-1705), who brought as a part of her dowry the island of Bombay which was to become a principal seat of British power in India. Miniature by Cooper

agitations and tumults, but in the main fought with words. In them the opposing sides gradually took on the aspect of political parties, loosely organized, but recognizable as distinctive groups. Within a generation, the Country Party and the Court Party, as they were called, were using the historic names of Whig and Tory about one another, although at first merely as terms of abuse. Amid many different pressures and complicated intrigues, the long tradition of government by two alternating parties saw its origins under Charles II.

Over this scene there presided a tall, dark, saturnine figure, gifted with a sceptical wit, a talent for dissimulation and an amorous disposition. In his youth, King Charles had fought for his Crown and narrowly escaped the clutches of his father's executioners. Many years of impoverished exile had followed and, on his restoration at the age of thirty, Charles was resolved to enjoy his own again and never more to depart on his travels. He succeeded in both parts of his purpose. A line of celebrated royal mistresses attests to his enjoyment of life, at least within a certain sphere, and the easy dethronement of his brother

231 In September 1666, near London Bridge, the GREAT FIRE broke out that swept the whole City, destroying thirteen thousand houses, eighty-nine churches and the old cathedral of St Paul's. The rebuilding that followed gave Sir Christopher Wren his architectural opportunity

and successor in 1688 proves some skill on Charles's part in avoiding the same fate.

Scepticism and Dissent

During Charles II's reign the Court presented a spectacle of scandal and frivolity, commemorated for future ages in the diaries of Pepys and Evelyn, the couplets of Dryden and the bawdy comedies of Restoration drama. The diarists also reflect, however, the serious political problems of the times through which Charles adroitly picked his way, aided by ministers to whom he left the main burdens of state, but in none of whom he placed his whole trust. For if a large part of the Court wore a cynical air, forces of religious conviction were nevertheless profoundly influential. Puritanism had lost control of the government, but in the country it ran deep. The age that, to the delight of the King and his friends, satirized the Puritans in the mock heroics of *Hudibras* was also one in which *Paradise Lost* and *The Pilgrim's Progress* were published. Milton, who had been Latin Secretary to the Council of State under Cromwell, and defended its actions in magniloquent pamphlets, lived out his years in blindness and obscurity, an abiding witness in his sonorous verses to the strength of Puritan tradition.

Milton is also a witness to the policy of toleration that it was Charles's object to pursue. Before his return, Charles had promised to observe the 'liberty of tender consciences', and after his accession he displayed a forbearance toward his father's former enemies that aroused dissatisfaction among the old Cavaliers. His first Parliament had shown itself more royalist than the King and had passed, in reactionary fervour, a number of laws imposing disabilities on the Puritan persuasion. One of them was an Act of Uniformity that had an effect opposite to its intention. Some two thousand ministers objected to the episcopal ordination required of them by this law, and withdrew from the Church of England, taking their congregations with them. They came to be known as Nonconformists or Dissenters. Through their action and their steadfastness of belief, Puritanism was transformed and channelled into the Nonconformist churches that have ever since exercised a notable influence, both fertile and restraining, upon English life and thought.

The Catholic Crux

There was another side to the religious medal—the Catholic one. The Roman Catholic minority in England had clung to its faith since the days of Queen Elizabeth, undaunted by official proscriptions. But now a Catholic wind was blowing at court. The heir to the throne, James, Duke of York, and a number of men and women of some station, were converted to Catholicism. The King himself looked favourably upon Catholics and wished to extend toleration towards them as well as to Dissenters. In his secret negotiations with Louis XIV, he even promised to re-establish Catholicism as the national religion. Whether such a realist among kings as Charles ever meant to carry out his intention may be in doubt. In effect, the result of his diplomacy was to secure a financial subsidy from King Louis that helped him to maintain some independence of Parliament while surrendering the direction of English foreign policy into French hands. Louis was free to attack the Dutch; Charles was strengthened in the struggle over

232 **THE PINEAPPLE PICTURE** by Henry Danckerts. Charles II, attended by spaniels, is offered the first pineapple grown in England by the royal gardener at Dawnay Court, Surrey

233 **The brilliance and gaiety of the Restoration theatre were graced by the first appearance of actresses; among them NELL GWYNN (1650-87), who bore the King two sons. Portrait by Lely**

Catholicism that pre-occupied the 1670's and over the position of his Catholic brother and heir.

Alarmed by the movement towards Catholicism, Parliament in 1673 passed a Test Act, excluding Roman Catholics from holding office under the Crown. But what if the Crown itself were Catholic? Protestant feeling was genuinely stirred at the prospect of the Duke of York's succession. It was also artificially whipped up by the fabrication of a 'Popish Plot' said to involve the assassination of the King. All this was wild illusion, but it exacerbated the national temper. In Parliament the radical Protestant opposition strove to exclude the Duke of York by law from the throne. Passions ran high, and, for a while, York had to take refuge in Holland. But Charles, who cared for little beyond his own pleasure, was staunch in his family loyalty. The Stuart dynasty meant something to his chill heart. Calling upon all his guile, patience and powers of finesse, he outmanoeuvred the opposition. The last five years of his reign saw an unexpected monarchical triumph. Charles's will prevailed and his Catholic brother succeeded him in February 1685. Except for one uprising in the West country, bloodily suppressed, the country surprisingly acquiesced.

A policy of toleration in religious matters under a Catholic monarch might have proved generally acceptable, for the principle of toleration

Whiping Heresy Out of Windsor Chaple.

A Jesuit Preaching against our Bible.

A Priest selling of Relicks by Auction.

A Preist hard very hard at Work.

234, 235, 236, 237 Playing cards, caricaturing Catholic priests during the period of the alleged 'Popish Plot' to murder the King and instigate a general massacre of Protestants

Plate X (opposite) Painted during his brief reign by Nicolas de Largilliere, JAMES II (1685-88), whose Roman Catholic policy and absolutist leanings led to his overthrow in the 'Glorious Revolution' of Whig memory

was under discussion among men of thought—it played a large part in the political philosophy now being formulated by John Locke and was to have a widespread influence in the years ahead. Moreover, there were many vicars of Bray, willing to turn their coats in politics as well as in religion, according to the prevailing weather. An astute and congenial king might have rallied to himself a formidable body of support among high Tories, Dissenters, Catholics and waverers. But James II had neither of these qualities. Obstinate, haughty, narrow, he drove headlong to destruction. It was not simply his indulgence of Catholics that undid him, and his appointment of them to important offices, but the suspicion that his avowals of toleration masked a resolve to restore Catholic supremacy. It was certain that he was using prerogative powers to overrule the laws of the land. It was likely—and broadly believed—that his aim was an absolutist monarchy on the French model. Within four years of his accession James had united against him all the main groupings in the country. When William of Orange landed at Torbay, by Whig invitation assuming the role of Protestant saviour, James crumpled and fled. A 'glorious Revolution' was seldom more painlessly enacted.

238   The daughter of Clarendon, ANNE HYDE (1637-71), first wife of James, Duke of York, was the mother of Queen Mary, wife of William III, and of Queen Anne. Portrait from Lely's studio

239   As Lord High Admiral, James II, when DUKE OF YORK, presided devotedly over the Navy and himself played a gallant part in actions against the Dutch. A portrait by Riley showing the Duke in wig and armour

240 (*opposite*) A natural son of Charles II, JAMES, DUKE OF MONMOUTH (1649-85), became the figure-head of the Protestant cause and on his father's death made a desperate attempt to seize the throne. Defeated at Sedgemoor he was executed on his uncle's orders, and his followers were harshly persecuted in the 'Bloody Assizes' by the notorious Judge Jeffreys

JAMES D: OF MONMOUTH.

The Cabal

241   The initials of Charles II's ministers between 1667 and 1674 formed the sinister word 'Cabal'. Sir Thomas CLIFFORD (1630-73), Secretary of State, was a Roman Catholic who committed suicide

242   The King's secret relations with Louis XIV were conducted by Henry Bennett, Earl of ARLINGTON (1618-85), who excelled in the art of observing and managing Charles' temper

243   Son of a royal favourite, and himself the King's chosen companion in his lighter hours, George Villiers, second Duke of BUCKINGHAM (1628-83), was the author of several comedies and burlesques

244   At one time a royal Minister, Anthony ASHLEY COOPER, Earl of Shaftesbury (1621-83), later became leader of the opposition to Romanism and of the popular movement to exclude the Duke of York

245   For twenty years the virtual ruler of Scotland, John Maitland, Duke of LAUDERDALE (1616-82), outlasted all his fellow members of the Cabal in the cynical service of his master

The diarists and the Navy

246   Industrious civil servant, diarist, keen car-
eerist, amateur of music, literature, science, and
lover of contemporary life, **SAMUEL PEPYS**
(1633-1703) was a typical representative of his
many-sided age

247   During the long naval conflict between Great Britain and the Dutch United Provinces for the
mercantile mastery of the seas, one of the most dramatic engagements was **THE FOUR DAYS'**
BATTLE waged off the eastern English coast in June 1666

248   Very different from his fellow diarist Pepys
was JOHN EVELYN (1620-1706), expert gardener, sober country gentleman and a learned and
prolific essayist on artistic and scientific subjects

249 (*below*) The British East India Company, founded with a small capital in 1600 by a group of
London merchants and financiers, was steadily increasing British overseas trade. This plate shows
seventeenth-century EAST INDIAMEN AT DEPTFORD

250 The last of the English polymaths, or men of universal learning, SIR CHRISTOPHER WREN (1632-1723), besides making deep researches into astronomy and mathematics, replanned London after the Great Fire and bequeathed to his country some of its noblest buildings. Bust by Edward Pierce

The age of Wren

251 Apart from their experiments in the grand manner, English architects have always excelled in the production of small domestic buildings. REDDITCH, at Broad Chalke in Wiltshire, the village that was once the home of the gifted memoralist, John Aubrey

252 Grinling Gibbons (1648-1720) worked as master wood-carver to the Crown from the reign of Charles II to that of George I, and collaborated with Wren in St Paul's. DETAIL OF A GRINLING GIBBONS BALUSTRADE

253 On the blackened ruins of the huge medieval church, Christopher Wren raised present-day ST PAUL'S. The foundation stone was laid in 1675; the cathedral was completed thirty-five years later

254　**Wren made notable contributions to both University cities. In Cambridge he designed the exquisite classical Library of Trinity College, Pembroke College Chapel and EMANUEL COLLEGE CHAPEL** (1668-73)

255   **JOHN DRYDEN** (1631-170⬛
successfully combined the function
of poet, dramatist and critic. ⬛
'Absolom and Achitophel' he produced a resounding satire on contemporary political life. His Shakes-
perian tragedy 'All for Love' is on⬛
of the finest of English poetic drama⬛

Writers
and musicians

256   Tinker's son and licensed la⬛
preacher, **JOHN BUNYAN** (162⬛
88) spent more than twelve years ⬛
prison after the restoration of th⬛
Stuart monarchy. It was during h⬛
imprisonment in Bedford gaol tha⬛
he composed 'The Pilgrim's Progress'. A drawing by R. White

257   The gaiety and laxity of th⬛
new age are reflected in Restoratio⬛
comedy. Among its chief exponent⬛
was **WILLIAM WYCHERLE**⬛
(1640?-1716), whose first comed⬛
'Love in a Wood' had won him th⬛
favour of a royal mistress

M.ᵣ Henry Purcell.

258   Englishmen of the seventeenth century were just as devoted to music as their Elizabethan predecessors. An outstanding composer was
HENRY PURCELL (1659-95), organist at Westminster Abbey for more than fifteen years

IX

WILLIAM OF ORANGE AND QUEEN ANNE

259 Triumphantly attired as a Roman Emperor, WILLIAM III, in Kneller's portrait, rides out of Margate, where he landed in 1697 after the conclusion of his long war with Louis XIV

The Glorious Revolution

The England that William of Orange invaded in 1688 was a country growing in commercial wealth, manufacture and overseas enterprise. An elegance of taste and sophistication of manners, that would become characteristic of the eighteenth century, were already beginning to pervade society. At the same time, a substratum of town-bred, middle-class ways of living was continually being reinforced. Although the conduct of state still lay in the hands of political magnates, based upon the support of country gentry and mercantile interests, the system they managed was never inflexible. It took time, luck and patronage, as well as talent and application, for an ordinary family to rise in station and join the ruling groups; yet this happened with increasing frequency. Rank, and the social privileges that went with it, were now more accessible to newcomers. Notions of democracy, such as had been held by some of Cromwell's soldiers, now ran underground at home, and only in the American colonies gained openly in persuasion. The way was not closed, however, to the growth of democratic ideas when the time came for their widespread adoption. One outstanding result of the 'Glorious Revolution' was to consolidate a method of limited representative government in Britain that could later be broadened in scope without further revolution.

260 **An able, courageous but aloof ruler, WILLIAM OF ORANGE, seen by candlelight on Schalcken's portrait, inspired respect among the British people, but never won their sympathy**

261 **Brought to the throne by the Whig Revolution, WILLIAM III (1688-1702) and MARY II (1688-94) are shown in a Dutch engraving, wearing their Coronation robes**

William of Orange owed the invitation that yielded him the throne mainly to the initiative of a group of Whigs, appalled by the birth of an unexpected son to James II and by the prospect of a perpetuated Catholic dynasty. Many Tories were alarmed at the idea of breaking the legitimate succession, although most of them concurred in the compromise by which William and his wife Mary, James's daughter, were proclaimed joint sovereigns. This transfer of the Crown was accompanied by a Parliamentary Declaration of Rights, circumscribing royal powers, and by the grant of a considerable degree of toleration for Dissenters. Catholic disabilities, however, remained in force until the nineteenth century.

King William III showed little liking for the kingdoms he had thus acquired, and his new subjects reciprocated his feelings. His heart was wholly in the struggle with France that had long overshadowed his native Netherlands and was now for nearly ten years also to engulf England. The war, fought in the Netherlands, at sea, and against King James in Ireland, came to no resounding conclusion, but it had a number of aspects and results important for the future: James was beaten at the Battle of the Boyne; the Protestant succession was secured in the British isles and French ambitions in Europe were decisively, although momentarily, checked. The war demonstrated the capacity of a coalition between England and her continental allies to withstand the most powerful and menacing of European states—a lesson that was to be repeated more than once—and it again proved the value to England of preserving command of the seas. At the same time it bore witness to the financial strength of the thriving British isles, now symbolized in the newly-founded Bank of England. As London grew to be the financial capital of the world, the country's range of influence on the international scene grew with it.

The Age of Anne

On the death of King William in 1702, the sovereign who succeeded, as Parliament had prescribed, was his sister-in-law, Anne. Although the last Stuart monarch was perhaps the least gifted of her line, she was also the least flawed by her family's notorious failings. As Queen, she had the fortune to lend her name to an epoch that was splendid and outstanding in many spheres of achievement, and a large number of its nobler monuments remain for admiration today.

Since the Great Fire of London in 1666, the skyline of the City had gradually been transformed by the architectural genius of Sir Christopher Wren, displayed in the spires and towers of his fifty-two churches and in the great dome of Saint Paul's Cathedral, which was still building in Anne's reign. Outside the City itself, and in all parts of England, town houses and country seats were rising in the beautifully proportioned stone and redbrick style that became characteristic of the age. If buildings reflect both the elegance and solidity of the period,

262　Kensington Palace, built on the rural outskirts of the capital, was one of the favourite residences of William III. Designed by Sir Christopher Wren, the ORANGERY at Kensington stands in what is now one of London's central parks, a witness to the age's taste for exotic fruits

its intellectual curiosity and refinement of mind found notable expression in science and literature. Sir Isaac Newton, his revolutionary contributions to physics already recognized, presided over the Royal Society, founded in Charles II's reign for the 'improvement of natural knowledge', and now at full lustre. In literature, both prose and verse began to acquire a new suppleness and delicacy, and prose, at least, extended its range to every subject worth the notice of an intelligent reader. Periodical writing multiplied and the first English newspapers started to circulate. News of affairs and instant comment upon them were beginning to spread far beyond the old circles within which they had been confined.

Against this rapidly changing background the political disputes and combinations of Whig and Tory, and of many subtler shades of allegiance in between the extremes, followed the pattern laid down by the Revolution of 1689. The sovereign was obliged to pay close attention to Whig principles, which contained the seeds of future liberal tradition, and often to accept governments that were largely Whiggish in complexion. But the Tories presented less of a threat to royal powers, which, although shorn, was still considerable. The Tories, moreover, were generally firm supporters of the Church of England, and particularly of the High Church party in it, with which the throne was closely identified. For most of her reign Queen Anne depended upon Tory-led administrations, although the issues of moment led to many Whig inroads and interludes of coalition.

263 and 264 **To Henry VIII's Tudor palace at HAMPTON COURT, fifteen miles west of London, William and Mary made splendid additions. Wren built for them FOUNTAIN COURT which contained the royal apartments. The OVERMANTEL, in relief, is the work of the Flemish artist, John Nost**

The country in 1702 was committed to a war that engaged almost the whole of Europe and lasted for eleven years. It was the supreme struggle with the great monarch in Versailles, whose will and ambition had long been to control the affairs of the continent. His opportunity came when the childless Hapsburg king of Spain died, leaving his throne to Louis XIV's grandson. This meant that the Bourbon family would rule not only over Spain, but over Belgium, half of Italy, and a very large part of the New World, stretching from the Gulf of St. Lawrence and California to the tip of South America. For Britain, Holland and the Hapsburg Emperor in Vienna, who had claims of his own to Spain, Louis XIV's acceptance of the Spanish empire on behalf of his grandson represented an intolerable accumulation of power that had to be resisted and broken. Louis would not listen to terms, and the 'Grand Alliance' went to war.

The campaigns that followed convulsed Spain, Italy and Germany, and also influenced the future of North America, but the heart of the struggle lay in Belgium. No English government could countenance the prospect of Belgium, then the Spanish Netherlands, being in the hands of a hostile power. From this cockpit of Europe, as it became and remained, the military genius of John Churchill, Duke of Marlborough, dominated the fields of war. Marlborough had proved his abilities in battle under James II and William III. Now, as the Allies' chief commander, he rose to world stature. His long career of victory— Blenheim, Ramillies and Oudenarde are among the British battle honours due to him—has few parallels in modern military history. What steadily eluded him was the conclusion of a victorious peace. After nine years of continuous action, the rise of a new favourite at court, and the appointment of a fresh combination of Ministers, led to his dismissal.

The nation was weary of war, and peace negotiations followed. By the Treaty of Utrecht in 1713, the Spanish inheritance was partitioned

---

265 The last of the Stuart sovereigns, QUEEN ANNE (1702-14) presided over a magnificent epoch in British history: portrait of the Princess before her accession, by Dahl, showing her with her son William, who died in childhood. 266 On a ceiling at Hampton Court she is depicted by Verrio, enthroned as JUSTICE

267 Built to commemorate Marlborough's famous victory in 1704, BLENHEIM PALACE, near Oxford, was designed by the playwright and architect, Sir John Vanbrugh. It has remained the seat of the Marlborough family, and Sir Winston Churchill was born there in 1874. The north front

arah wife to Iohn Duke
f Marlborough.

between Bourbon and Hapsburg. A framework of European relations was established that endured until the French Revolution overturned the old diplomatic world. Britain—and the island name is constitutionally now accurate, since the Act of Union between England and Scotland was sealed in Queen Anne's reign—Britain gained advantages overseas: the possession of Gibraltar and Minorca as naval bases, and of Nova Scotia and Newfoundland in the Canada, then largely French, that was gradually to acquire a British orientation. Henceforth, until the climate of opinion changed in the twentieth century, successful participation in European wars meant for Britain colonial and commercial expansion. The first imperial age was dawning that was to meet its challenge, and reluctantly accept its defeat, at the hands of its own North American foundations.

268 Queen Anne's Catholic half-brother, **PRINCE JAMES FRANCIS EDWARD STUART** (1688-1766), was later known to his Jacobite supporters as 'King James III', but to most Englishmen as 'The Old Pretender'. Painted at the age of seven with his sister, Louisa, by Nicolas de Largillière

Plate XI (*opposite*) **The close friend and confidante of the Queen, SARAH CHURCHILL, DUCHESS OF MARLBOROUGH** (1660-1744) exerted an immense influence on public affairs and faithfully represented her husband's interests while he was at the wars. Portrait by Kneller

269   For ten years Queen Anne's commander-in-chief, JOHN CHURCHILL, DUKE OF MARLBOROUGH (1650-1722), was virtually the leader of the European coalition against France. Among his notable victories was OUDENARDE, fought in Flanders in 1708. A tapestry at Blenheim shows Marlborough carrying his baton and surrounded by his staff

270 At one time Marlborough's supporter, ROBERT HARLEY (1661-1724), when he became chief minister, dismissed the Duke from office and concluded the much criticized Treaty of Utrecht that put an end to the wars

Men of state

271 An accomplished politician, SIDNEY GODOLPHIN (1645-1712) was for eight years Lord High Treasurer and, until he fell from royal favour, Marlborough's staunch political ally. Bust by Rysbrack

272 Harley's brilliant rival for leadership, Henry St John, VISCOUNT BOLINGBROKE (1678-1751) compromised himself in the Jacobite cause and for a time became secretary to the exiled 'Old Pretender'

Country houses

273　Thanks to Inigo Jones, the classical tradition in architecture had now developed strong roots. CHATSWORTH, built for the Duke of Devonshire by William Talman, who completed his work in 1696

274 **The smaller houses of the age had their own solid unobtrusive dignity. MOMPESSON HOUSE, in the Close of Salisbury Cathedral, a modest but extremely elegant structure, dates from the year 1701**

275 **Dutch gables appeared on many unpretentious rural buildings, particularly in the eastern counties where Dutch engineers had been engaged to drain the water-logged fens. The WHITE HART INN, SCOLE, Norfolk**

277 (*below*) **In WARBROOK, EVERSLEY, which he had designed for himself, John James, one-time assistant to Sir Christopher Wren, settled down to spend his last days after he had retired from practice**

276 (*left*) **During the reign of William of Orange, Dutch influence coloured the work of English architects. CHICHELEY HALL, with its beautiful south front, was designed for a family that had recently returned from Holland**

A
Weekly Review
OF THE
Affairs of *FRANCE*:

Purg'd from the Errors and Partiality of *News-Writers* and *Petty-Statesmen*, of all Sides.

𝕾𝖆𝖙𝖚𝖗𝖉𝖆𝖞, Feb. 19. 1704.

The INTRODUCTION.

THIS Paper is the Foundation of a very large and useful Defign, which, if it meet with fuitable Encouragement, *Permiffu Superiorum*, may contribute to Setting the Affairs of *Europe* in a Clearer Light, and to prevent the various uncertain Accounts, and the Partial Reflections of our Street-Scriblers, who Daily and Monthly Amufe Mankind with Stories of Great Victories when we are Beaten, Miracles when we Conquer, and a Multitude of Unaccountable and Inconfiftent Stories, which have at leaft this Effect, That People are poffeft with wrong Notions of Things, and Nations Wheedled to believe Nonfenfe and Contradiction.

278   Novelist, journalist and versatile pamphleteer, **DANIEL DEFOE** (1659?-1731), in addition to his political and commercial activities, was the story-teller of imaginative genius who created 'Robinson Crusoe' and 'Moll Flanders'

279   **DEFOE'S 'REVIEW'**, an eight-page weekly journal, dealing with current affairs in Europe, of which this is the first issue, was largely written by the industrious editor himself. It ran from February 1704 to June 1713

Men of letters
and learning

280   The new type of social comedy that had flowered on the Restoration stage was brought to perfection by **WILLIAM CONGREVE** (1670-1729), whose masterpiece, the enchanting 'Love for Love', was first presented in 1695

281   The literary career of **JONATHAN SWIFT** (1667-1745) began with 'The Battle of the Books' in 1697; but he scored his greatest triumph, as a master of modern prose, with the publication of 'Gulliver's Travels' in 1726

145

282 Journalism, as we understand it today, gradually emerged during the age of Anne. A versatile and accomplished editor was SIR RICHARD STEELE (1672-1729), who launched the 'Tatler' in 1709 and the 'Spectator' in 1711

283 Steele's friend and collaborator, JOSEPH ADDISON (1672-1719) was among the first of modern literary journalists, the author of felicitous occasional essays in which he commented with airy elegance upon the contemporary scene

284 On his tomb in Westminster Abbey, SIR ISAAC NEWTON (1642-1727) personifies the scientific spirit. Philosopher, physicist, mathematician, President from 1703 of the Royal Society, he formulated the law of gravitation and the laws of motion

Social life and commerce

'COUNTRY LIFE'

285   Rich business men were constantly swelling the ranks of the landed aristocracy. SIR JOSIAH CHILD, here represented in monumental full dress, was a merchant of the City of London whose son and heir obtained an earldom

286   The scientific interests of the age extended both to abstruse discoveries and to the construction of ingenious mechanical devices—such as JOHN LOFTING'S FIRE ENGINE (1690). In the background stands London's Royal Exchange

287 and 288   Children continued to wear adult dress, as they had done in previous centuries. These statues, from the front of a seventeenth-century London school, show a SCHOOL-GIRL and SCHOOL-BOY in the reign of Anne

289   English seamen still emulated the daring of their Elizabethan ancestors. WILLIAM DAMPIER (1652-1715) sailed the Atlantic and Pacific both as an explorer and as a privateer. In 1701 he returned from an expedition to Australia

290   Few publishers have been able to boast of so distinguished a list as JACOB TONSON (1656?-1736). His authors included Milton (whose 'Paradise Lost' he and his brother purchased), Dryden, Addison, Steele and Pope

X

THE HOUSE OF HANOVER

291 The first of the Hanoverian line, who was always more deeply interested in the affairs of his German Electorate than in his new kingdom, GEORGE I (1714-27), portrayed by Rysbrack. During his reign the long rule of the Whigs began

'When George in pudding times came o'er,' landing at Greenwich on September 18, 1714, he found the great majority of his subjects favourably disposed towards their new ruler, whose advent ensured the Protestant succession, which they believed would bring the country peace. Descended from James I through his grandmother, the Electress Sophia, he had been recognized as heir to Queen Anne under the provisions of the Act of Settlement in 1701. The English governing class welcomed a sovereign who appeared to have few political ambitions; for George I, who knew very little English, seldom intervened in the daily conduct of affairs and was chiefly concerned with keeping the throne that he and his family had inherited. He was glad to leave the general management of the kingdom to the group of powerful noblemen, the landed gentry and the sprinkling of rich commercialists who now dominated the English scene; and it was they whose influence and interests shaped the development of the new age. In 1715, and again in 1745, the House of Stuart attempted to recover their heritage. But both Jacobite risings collapsed; the Hanoverian dynasty remained unshaken; and England embarked on a period of prosperous growth that was to continue for more than a hundred years.

The Royal Family

Not that the Hanoverians were particularly popular monarchs. Flanked by two grotesque German mistresses and followed by his Turkish body-servants, George I, when he arrived, cut an alien and unattractive figure. Brought up as a petty foreign prince, he clung to his previous tastes and habits. 'No man was every more free from ambition,' writes Lady Mary Wortley-Montagu. 'He was more properly dull than lazy.' Of his son, the future George II, the same writer gives a different, but equally unprepossessing, sketch: 'The fire of his temper appeared in every look and gesture. . . . He was naturally sincere, and his pride told him that he was placed above restraint'; so that he regarded 'all the men and women he saw as creatures he might kiss or kick for his diversion'. His wife, Caroline of Ansbach, was, it is true, one of the cleverest women of her time. But Caroline practised the difficult art of governing by seeming to obey and submit; and when she exerted her authority, she did so through her ally Sir Robert Walpole, who soon became the King's chief minister. With their son, Frederick Prince of Wales, both his parents were on extremely bad terms. Just as George II had quarrelled with George I, Frederick rebelled against his father and, like his grandson, afterwards George

292 **GEORGE II (1727-60) at the battle of Dettingen in 1743 was the last English king to fight at the head of his troops**, an action here commemorated in the painting by John Wootton. Britain in these years enjoyed increasing prosperity and a steady expansion overseas. If the King contributed little to the age save valour, his consort **QUEEN CAROLINE**, 293 (*right*), was 'curious in everything', and 'wrote and conversed' on more topics than the average educated man

IV, he added insult to injury by joining the ranks of his father's political opponents.

The first Prime Minister

The first 'Prime Minister' to reside at 10 Downing Street was Sir Robert Walpole, whose ascendancy spanned two reigns from 1721 to 1742. Walpole's foes had originally coined the title as an indication of the ruthless skill with which he managed and dominated his fellow-ministers; but thanks to the success with which he pursued his policies, it presently took on a much less critical meaning and eventually became attached to every leader of a British government. Above all, Walpole was a man of peace; and the long *Pax Walpoliana*, during which Great Britain managed to steer clear of European conflicts and commitments, lasted for nearly two decades. At home, he excelled in financial affairs and helped to launch the country he governed on a long period of triumphant commercial expansion. Thanks to his efforts, London established her place as the mercantile centre of modern Europe. Among contemporary politicians, however, his reputation was unenviable. Persuaded that 'every man had his price', he maintained his power by a widespread system of bribery. A genuine patriot and a far-sighted national leader, he was also a good-natured cynic. Despite his passion for the arts—he built himself a splendid country house and stocked it with magnificent objects—he remained in his private existence a bluff, hard-drinking Norfolk squire.

Social Life

When the contemporaries of Johnson, Gibbon and Burke looked back on the early eighteenth century, they found it coarse and uncultivated almost to the point of barbarism; and indeed, as Hogarth's pictures show, it had its harsh forbidding aspects. But the harshness of the age was redeemed by its abounding masculine vigour. The Walpolian age and the age that immediately followed it were periods of rapid growth.

295 (*opposite*) **SIR ROBERT WALPOLE** (1676-1745) depicted with some of his hounds by John Wootton, followed the pursuits of a country gentleman throughout his long tenure of office as 'Prime Minister'. His hold over the House of Commons and his skill in eliminating rivals to his power have scarcely been matched in parliamentary history. While his financial ability brilliantly served the state, he also amassed a personal fortune that enabled him to build magnificently at **HOUGHTON HALL** 294 (*left*) The architect was Colen Campbell, and William Kent was among those employed on the decoration

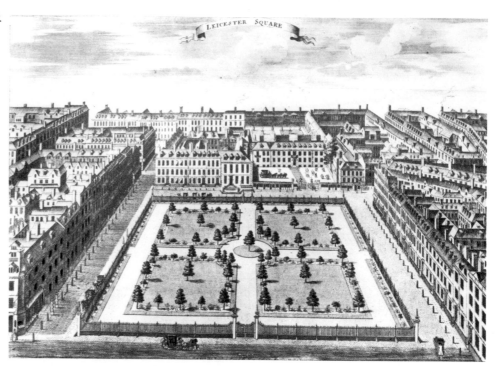

LEICESTER SQUARE

296 **One of the new residential squares of Hanoverian London; LEICESTER SQUARE, at the end of which stands Leicester House, where George II before his accession and Frederick Prince of Wales held 'opposition' courts**

Not only did the English ruling classes continue to increase their wealth and power, but the gentry and rising middle class reached a new level of prosperity and comfort. Hogarth, the foremost painter of his day and the greatest of all 'pictorial dramatists', besides exploring the London underworld and illustrating the tragedies of vice and crime, produced a long series of brilliant conversation pieces in which respectable citizens are shown at their ease against a dignified domestic background. Meanwhile London, the focus of English wealth, was beginning to assume its present shape. Since many of the older parts of the city had been totally destroyed by the great fire of 1666 and gradually rebuilt on more graceful and more spacious lines, Hanoverian London, as a whole, had an agreeably trim and modern look, with its new churches, its solid mercantile streets and the elegantly proportioned aristocratic squares that were beginning to spread out across the open fields in what is now the West End.

Wren had been succeeded by William Kent, an artist of lesser genius but no less energy; and with the support of his gifted patron, the patrician dilettante Lord Burlington, he introduced a vogue for Palladian architecture that produced many notable English buildings. But the most original artist of the age was unquestionably William Hogarth, who ridiculed Kent and Burlington, and prided himself on his staunchly English character. He survived until 1764; but much of his finest work was carried out before the middle of the century. It reflects the strength, the gusto, the sanguine self-confidence of early eighteenth-century England.

297 **WILLIAM HOGARTH** (1697-1764),
modelled in terracotta by Roubiliac, was
the son of a schoolmaster and began his
prolific career as an engraver's apprentice.
Among his striking delineations of the age
were the series of moral satires painted and
engraved in 1745, showing, 298 (*below*), **the
vicissitudes of MARIAGE A LA MODE**

Hanoverian London

299 (*above*) **Antonio Canaletto (1697-1768) painted for ten years in London, suffusing his vision of the scene in Venetian sunlight. His prospect of WHITEHALL FROM RICHMOND HOUSE shows Charles I's Banqueting House in the centre and the Tudor Treasury Gate on the left**

300 (*below*) **Although the power of the Whig magnates was based on their country connections, town houses were the centres for their political operations: NEWCASTLE HOUSE in Lincoln's Inn Fields**

301 **The manner of Wren was continued and developed in the buildings of James Gibbs (1682-1754), a keen student of Roman architecture, whose ST MARTIN-IN-THE-FIELDS has become one of the best-sited churches in London since the opening of Trafalgar Square**

Plate XII   Greenwich has been associated with the Royal Navy since the days of Henry VIII. Canaletto's view of the ROYAL NAVAL HOSPITAL from across the Thames shows the buildings of Inigo Jones, and of Wren and his successors, as they appeared in the mid-eighteenth century. Today they house the Royal Naval College and the National Maritime Museum

In and out of Parliament

302   The **HOUSE OF COMMONS** had now become the main arena in the political struggle; here Arthur Onslow (1691-1768) presides as Speaker, exchanging a word with Walpole

303   **Courtier and man - of - letters, JOHN, LORD HERVEY** (1696-1743) was the author of the vividly satiric 'Memoirs of the Reign of George II'. His portrait comes from the studio of the French artist, J. B. Vanloo

304   **Few mid-Georgian administrations were formed without the help of the DUKE OF NEWCASTLE** (1693-1768), an anxious magnifico who was more successful at managing elections than in the control of national policy. A portrait by William Hoare

305   **English liberties** were thought to be endangered by Walpole's contentious Excise Bill. The Prime Minister is cartooned, drawn by a dejected lion and unicorn, mounted on a hogshead of tobacco and riding down Magna Carta; **EXCISE IN TRIUMPH, 1733**

306   **In Hogarth's picture CANVASSING FOR VOTES, a farmer is bribed by the agents of both parties outside an inn**

307   **The Jacobite invasion of 1745. In THE HIGHLAND CHASE the Duke of Cumberland pursues Charles Edward**

Empire-builders

308   Under the leadership of ROBERT CLIVE (1725-74), the British East India Company defeated the French and their Indian allies, and acquired in the province of Bengal the foundation for the British Raj. Portrait by N. Dance

309   By his daring capture of Quebec, GENERAL JAMES WOLFE (1726-59) opened the way towards a British dominion in Canada. He fell in the moment of victory, and this portrait is posthumous

10 The elder William Pitt, later EARL OF CHATHAM (1708-78), organised the series of victories in Europe, Canada and India that marked the Seven Years War with France. He is portrayed in a picture from the studio of W. Hoare during his years as the 'Great Commoner', when his position depended on his personal ascendancy in Parliament. Distrusted by George III, he became on his resignation in 1761 THE DISTRESSED STATESMAN, 311 *(right)*, of the cartoonist

312   The poetic giant of the early eighteenth century, **ALEXANDER POPE** (1688-1744) was in life a dwarfish invalid. Already famous during the age of Anne, he composed his masterpiece, 'Moral Essays', between 1731 and 1735. The bust is by Roubiliac

313   **SAMUEL RICHARDSON** (1689-1761), novelist, printer, publisher, may claim with Defoe to have originated the modern novel. Joseph Highmore (1692-1780) painted his portrait two years after the publication of 'Clarissa'

314   The eighteenth-century artists usually needed an aristocratic patron—like the plump poetaster whom Hogarth displays, enthusiastically reading his verses aloud to **LORD GEORGE GRAHAM** in his cabin

315   In an age of easy-going bishops and comfortable ecclesiastical sinecures, JOHN WESLEY (1703-91), founder of Methodism, carried his fiery devotional message up and down the whole country

316   The hope of the exiled House of Stuart, CHARLES EDWARD, THE YOUNG PRETENDER (1720-88) led the abortive Jacobite rising of 1745. Forty-three years later, he died in Italy a broken and exhausted man

Men of the age

317   Hogarth earned fame with his conversation pieces before he embarked upon his 'pictorial dramas'. LORD CHOLMONDELEY AND HIS FAMILY is an excellent example of the painter in his most domestic vein

Great houses

and colleges

319 (*below*) **As the rich rose in the social scale they acquired houses of appropriate size and grandeur, such as WANSTEAD (1715-22) built by Sir Richard Child, later Earl Tylney, heir to a family of successful merchants**

318 **Completed in 1763, WEST WYCOMBE PARK was the home of Sir John Dashwood, a founding member of the Hell Fire Club, who combined a thirst for dissipation with an interest in the liberal arts**

320 James Gibbs, architect of St. Martin-in-the-Fields, constructed RAGLEY HALL for a discerning patron between 1750 and 1755. This magnificent fireplace decorates the entrance hall

321 Wren's associated and favourite pupil, Nicholas Hawksmoor (1661-1736), by 1720 had made this arresting addition to the variegated Oxford sky-line—the boldly gothicized towers of ALL SOUL'S COLLEGE

322 (*below*) Besides exercising his talents as a letter-writer, Horace Walpole—Sir Robert's third son—became a celebrated dilettante. In 1747 he bought an estate near the Thames, renamed his property STRAWBERRY HILL, 323 (*right*), and embarked on the construction of a 'little Gothic castle', which reveals the growing taste for romantic and exotic detail

'COUNTRY LIFE'

Country life

324 Gainsborough's early portrait of MR AND MRS ANDREWS was probably painted as a wedding
present. Behind them stretch the fields and woods of Suffolk—the beloved landscape of the painter's youth

325 **In this picture of a country gentleman and hounds, Wootton's chief subject is HENRY HOARE OF STOUR-HEAD, whose beautifully landscaped gardens and park contained a grotto with a lyrical inscription by Pope**

326 **A squire in the north of England commissioned this four-fold PAINTED SCREEN, with its graphic representations of the country pastimes he himself preferred—from hunting and cockfighting to gambling and swimming. It was executed about 1746**

Leisure and entertainment

327   'A bold, Irish-faced girl', off-spring of a Dublin bricklayer, PEG WOFFINGTON (1714?-60) was renowned as the handsomest actress who had ever performed upon the English stage. She excelled in masculine roles, or 'breeches' parts

328   (*below*) Of the numerous pleasure-gardens that enlivened the outskirts of London, none was more fashionable than RANELAGH. The interior of its central rotunda was commemorated by Canaletto during his visit to England

329   Prosperous members of the London professional class, MR OLDHAM AND HIS FRIENDS, gather to talk and smoke and drink. It was Joseph Highmore who recorded for posterity this agreeable occasion

30 **FREDERICK PRINCE OF WALES AND HIS SISTERS** enjoy a musical party in their private apartments at Windsor Castle. Frederick's love of music seems to have been one of his few redeeming features

XI

AMERICAN INDEPENDENCE

The Background

to the Struggle

Until the second half of the eighteenth century, the fortunes of America had been little affected by European crises, except in so far as Indian wars were prompted by Anglo-French hostility. At the price of remaining a part of the British system, the colonies grew up guarded from world events. But their future was profoundly influenced by the third of the period's great wars between Britain and France, and especially by the British 'Year of Victory' in 1759.

In that year, Quebec fell to Wolfe, and French power on the continent was broken, not only in Canada but along the Ohio Valley and throughout the Mississippi basin. By the Peace of Paris, all the territories between the Appalachians and the Mississippi passed under the British Crown. Their control now became one of the many items in dispute between the colonists and the King's government during the uneasy years that preceded the shot at Lexington that was heard round the world. Whatever London might proclaim, the result of this vast acquisition was to be the opening of the Middle West to American enterprise, and the certainty, in the course of time, that North America would become overwhelmingly English-speaking. Such was William

331 This view of FORT GEORGE WITH THE CITY OF NEW YORK in colonial times, with British flags prominent, was probably drawn by a visiting naval officer in the 1730s

332 The PENNSYLVANIA JOURNAL in 1765 warns its subscribers that the Stamp Act will oblige it to cease publication. This British revenue law led to the first effective demonstration of colonial opposition in America

Pitt's legacy to the Americans, commemorated in the renaming of the former French Fort Duquesne, which was henceforth Pittsburg.

The removal of the French menace from the hinterland of the colonies had other far-reaching effects. It helped quicken the pace towards thoughts of independence. British troops, stationed on American soil, now no longer seemed essential to the safety of the colonists, and difficulties over their quartering and supply gave rise to angry grievances. So, too, did the question of paying for them. Broad issues clustered round this point, for which there were no commonly established solutions. The problems estranging Britain and America, which involved the cost of defence, the control of trade and manufacture and the power to tax and coin money, were both interrelated and unsettled.

334 The leader of the Massachusetts radicals
and political organizer of the Revolution in
New England, SAMUEL ADAMS (1722-1803)
is portrayed by his accomplished fellow Boston-
ian, John Singleton Copley

333 A distinguished American por-
traitist of the revolutionary age was
Charles Willson Peale (1741-1827) who
here depicts WASHINGTON AFTER
THE CAMPAIGN OF TRENTON AND
PRINCETON, his successful winter
actions in New Jersey, 1776-77

What contribution should the colonies make to the imperial exchequer in London? Where was the just dividing line between taxes voted by the local assemblies and those, including customs dues, that had hitherto been ordained by London? How could the diversifying economic interests of the colonies be reconciled with the objects of British policy? Overshadowing these anxieties lay the constitutional dilemma by which the sovereign Parliament at Westminster found itself in conflict with the representatives of colonial opinion. There was no precedent for consultation as between equals. Even a statesman so sympathetic to the American cause as Burke considered that Parliament in Britain had indisputable powers of superintendence over colonial legislatures, while these, on their side, naturally resented the inferior place allotted them in the eighteenth-century imperial connection.

During the decade of debate before independence, the colonies asked only for the same traditional English rights as the King's subjects enjoyed in Britain. They thought it natural to appeal to George III against the actions of his Ministers and Parliament. The more moderate among them hoped that the Crown would be impartial in what was still a series of quarrels between the two groups of its subjects. It was a hope never to be realized, although King George's personal obstinacy was only in part at fault. His role, as villain of the piece, was cast for him in American patriotic literature and English Whig polemics. His misfortune remains that he seemed to fill it so well. But, in fact, during the 1770s the King simply shared and supported his Ministers' views.

335 **The numerous loyalists in the colonies were objects of scorn to the radicals. Here TORIES ARE HUNG IN EFFIGY at Lebanon, Connecticut**

And they never had difficulty in securing majorities in Parliament until after the war had been lost. The struggle between Britain and America began as a contest over the balance of power within the existing framework. Time sharpened it into a struggle between opposing systems.

The War and its Outcome

Was the Anglo-American clash inevitable? Every Revolution acquires an aura of inevitability once it has happened. But where is the point to be fixed from which there was no return? The record of America's dynamic growth suggests that sooner or later a break with Britain was bound to come. Destiny and tradition were pulling in opposite directions. Yet sixteen years elapsed between the furious troubles over the Stamp Act and the surrender at Yorktown. When did the split become irreparable?

On both sides of the Atlantic there were large bodies of opinion sympathetic with one another and eager for an accommodation. Not only the Whigs in Britain deplored the widening of the quarrel. In America, possibly as many as one-third of the colonists were 'loyal' for the greater part of the war. But in times of tension, it is extreme views on either side that harden the issue and define it beyond compromise. In London, the Ministers of the Crown, with the encouragement of their sovereign, grew stubbornly intent on teaching the colonists a lesson. This was not so much for the sake of 'imperialist' principles as because, like many wavering governments that feel themselves flouted, Lord North and his colleagues reached a moment when they found the evasion of their laws intolerable.

On the American side, there were always voices preaching the virtues of separation, although ready to maintain some kind of link. There were also active radicals, determined to provoke a revolutionary spark, to whom British blunders offered many opportunities for bringing a climate of civil war into existence. These they did not hesitate to seize; yet the process took years. It has been said that the American

336 Printer, journalist, philosopher, scientist, ambassador and statesman, BENJAMIN FRANKLIN (1706-90), in the limitless curiosity of his mind, seemed to typify to contemporaries on both sides of the Atlantic a new and original species of man—the American

337 The second President of the United States, JOHN ADAMS (1735-1826), who played an umpire's role amid the constitutional questions that vexed the making of his country. By Copley

Revolution was effected in the hearts and minds of the people long before the Declaration of Independence was issued. In a sense this is so, since the act of emigration is itself a revolution for any man or family. But the thoughtful leaders, who gave shape to the American republic, shared a widespread conservative instinct to keep some form of tie with the old world from which they had sprung. The American destiny was slow to be made manifest among most of the founding fathers of the United States.

Six years went by after the 'Boston Massacre' before the momentous Declaration issued from Philadelphia on July 4, 1776:

'When in the Course of human events, it becomes necessary for one people to dissolve the political bands which have connected them with another, and to assume among the Powers of the earth, the separate and equal station to which the Laws of Nature and of Nature's God entitle them, a decent respect to the opinions of mankind requires that they should declare the causes which impel them to the separation.

'We hold these truths to be self-evident, that all men are created equal, that they are endowed by their Creator with certain unalienable Rights, that among these are Life, Liberty, and the pursuit of Happiness. That to secure these rights, Governments are instituted among Men, deriving their just powers from the consent of the governed. That whenever any Form of Government becomes destructive of these ends, it is the Right of the People to alter or to abolish it, and to institute new Government, laying its foundation on such principles and organizing its powers in such form, as to them shall seem most likely to effect their Safety and Happiness.'

Plate XIII The British capitulation at Yorktown on October 17, 1781, to the forces of Washington and his French allies, marked the end of active warfare and, for America, the beginning of a new age. Peale's commemorative painting shows GEORGE WASHINGTON (1732-99) with the MARQUIS DE LAFAYETTE (1757-1834)

338 Towards the close of the eighteenth century; a view of PHILA-
DELPHIA, showing Second Street,
north from Market Street, with a view
of Christ Church; from a drawing by
William and Thomas Birch

Even after the 'Boston Tea Party', and the bloodshed at Breed's Hill and Lexington, civil war could have been ended if the British Commander had been given the power to treat with the Continental Congress. The opposing lines were not irrevocably drawn up. But London was both muddled and inflexible; America was increasingly exasperated, and civil war became a war of independence.

In America, the imponderables of a struggle for liberation soon made themselves felt. Increasingly divided counsels on the one side, and a growing sense of purpose on the other, played a conspicuous part. So did international luck. American disunity and lack of organization were matched by British military errors and ignorance of the conditions in which the campaigns were fought. At low moments in the war for the Americans, when it seemd as if their armies might dissolve overnight, a Trenton or a Saratoga rallied continental spirits. And these American successes in turn led to the alliances with France and Spain that transformed the revolutionary war into a world struggle. Money, arms and men from Britain's European enemies, and the breaking of the British command of the seas, combined to make Yorktown possible for America. 'Lafayette, we are here,' was a stirring but historically ironic acknowledgment by the United States in 1917 of their debt to the Bourbon desire for revenge on Britain in 1777. Human resolution in America, however, counted for more.

If the States, that were once colonies, owe much to the drafters of the Declaration of Independence, who gave a single cause to thirteen diverse aspirations, they remain in perpetual debt to the undaunted spirit and energy of their first Commander-in-Chief. George Washington survived defeat and withdrawal, and kept his dwindling army in the field during the dark days at Valley Forge, while the British disported themselves in the Continental capital which they had conquered with ease. Washington's achievement fails to be a miracle only because of his rock-like character and tireless ability. For Britain, her own mistakes and the intervention of the French may seem reason enough why the 'world turned upside down' for Cornwallis's army on the shores of Chesapeake Bay. But, for America, this was the triumph of the countless patriot hopes that were embodied in the persistent spirit of one man who outlasted every adversity. For George Washington, eight years of Presidency were to crown his career, but he had already earned the title of Father of his Country on October 19, 1781. Peace was to take time to compose, and many years more were needed for the making of the new nation's Constitution; yet the United States had been conceived in the years between Breed's Hill and Yorktown. Washington alone had made the conception possible.

339 **Except during the British occupation in 1777-78, Philadelphia was the American capital and seat of the Continental Congress. The STATE HOUSE, after a drawing by Peale**

Cities

and

houses

340   This **ROMANTIC VIEW OF BOSTON** reflects the city's legendary character. Soon after its foundation by the elder John Winthrop in 1635, it was already becoming a centre of the country's intellectual life

341   In 1670 English settlers under William Sayle established themselves beside the Ashley river, some miles from the site of modern **CHARLESTON**, where ten years later they founded the great metropolis of the South

342 **MOUNT VERNON** was George Washington's home from 1747 until his death. After he had inherited it in 1754, he made many additions to his graceful two-storeyed wooden house

4 This elegant group of buildings at **WOODBURY, CONNECTICUT**, though influenced by a orgian sense of style, demonstrates how successfully the new transatlantic civilization had begun create for itself a worthy architectural setting

343 The local architects of New England developed ingenious variations on the architecture of the old country, making, as this **CLAPBOARD HOUSE** shows, a clever use of wood where their English ancestors had built in stone or brick

345   (*above*) **HARVARD IN 1726,** when the great university was already ninety years old, having been founded in 1636 by a grant from the Massachusetts Bay Company, to which John Harvard's bequest was added two years later

346 (*below*) The scenery of the New World was still observed by American artists from a largely European point of view. They had not yet discovered its individual character. **IMAGINARY LANDSCAPE** of the eighteenth century

Universities and social life

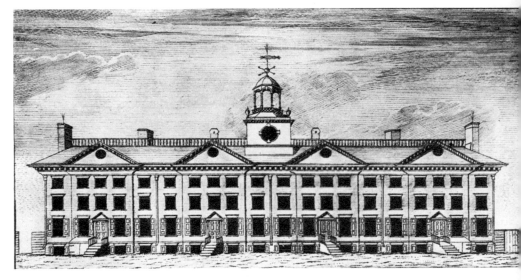

347 A royal grant founded **KING'S COLLEGE**, New York City, in 1754, which was re-opened as **COLUMBIA COLLEGE** after the American Revolution. A view of the buildings in 1760

348 **THE COLLEGE OF NEW JERSEY,** here shown in 1764, had received its original charter in 1746. The fourth colonial college to be established, it did not change its name to **PRINCETON** until the end of the nineteenth century

349 Among the traditional pursuits that the more affluent English settlers brought with them to their new American estates was the perilous sport of **FOX-HUNTING**. Picture painted about 1780

The American face

350 The Scottish-born painter, John Smibert (1688-1751) came to Rhode Island in the train of the philosopher, Bishop Berkeley, and stayed to record the features of the worthies of the age. His portrait of NATHANIEL BYFIELD

351 This portrait of AMOS DOOLITTLE is the work of the Connecticut artist, Ralph Earl (1751-1801), who specialized in painting news events and was one of the earliest recorders of the Battle of Lexington

352 Described by a contemporary diarist as 'the most extraordinary genius ever I knew', Robert Feke (1705?-1750) here portrays ISAAC WINSLOW, descendant of the famous New England family

353 John Singleton Copley (1738-1815), who spent his latter years in London, seems to have been equally at home on both sides of the Atlantic. This portrait of MRS JOHN AMORY was painted in 1763 before he left America

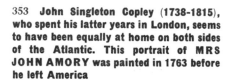

354   The American love of children is illustrated in the commissioning of many family portrait groups. The FOUR SALTER CHILDREN were painted by an unknown artist in the early years of the new Republic

355   The faces of the South are depicted in the paintings of the Swiss, Jeremiah Theus (c.1719-44), who settled in Charleston, South Carolina. His portrait of MRS GABRIEL MANIGAULT

356   The patrician faces of Dutch Americans look out from the canvases of the eighteenth century. This portrait of S. VAN RENSSELAER is attributed to Evert Duyckink III

357   Copley's gift of pictorial characterization was almost as highly developed as that of Hogarth. His COLONEL SPARHAWK radiates an air of genial affability and native shrewdness

War-leaders

358   The controversial victor at Saratoga, **MAJOR-GENERAL HORATIO GATES** (1727-1806) won a military reputation that his later actions in the Carolinas did not confirm. A drawing by John Trumbull

359   The liberator of Georgia and the Carolinas, **MAJOR-GENERAL NATHANAEL GREENE** (1742-86) lost his battles with Cornwallis but won the campaign. A portrait by Peale

360   Before he treacherously went over to the British in 1780, **MAJOR-GENERAL BENEDICT ARNOLD** (1741-1801) played an energetic part in the defence of the American north and helped to force Burgoyne's surrender

361   The mover of the congressional resolution on June 6, 1776, that 'these united colonies are, and of right ought to be, free and independent states', **RICHARD HENRY LEE** of Virginia (1732-94)

362 **The British commander-in-chief, who captured New York and occupied Philadelphia, but failed to press home his advantages against Washington's harassed army, LIEUTENANT-GENERAL SIR WILLIAM HOWE (1729-1814)**

364 **Forced to surrender to Washington at Yorktown after the French had gained command of the sea, Charles, MARQUESS CORNWALLIS (1738-1805), afterwards Governor-General of India. Portrait by Gainsborough**

363 (*left*) **A man of wit and fashion, with considerable military gifts, MAJOR-GENERAL JOHN BURGOYNE (1722-92) had the misfortune to lead the ambitious expedition from Canada that miscarried at Saratoga. Portrait by Reynolds**

The war on sea and river

365 (*above*) **Although as a Member of Parliament he had opposed the government's American policy, Lord Cornwallis served with distinction in the struggle that followed. CORNWALLIS LANDING TROOPS IN NEW JERSEY**

366 (*below*) **The American forces scored their first notable success with General Burgoyne's surrender at Saratoga in October 1777. BURGOYNE ON THE WEST BANK OF THE HUDSON**

Plate XIV **Naval hero of the Revolution, born near Kircudbright, Scotland, one-time chief mate on a slave-ship, Paul Jones (1747-92) carried the war against Great Britain far into European waters. This engraving, after a picture by Patton, illustrates PAUL JONES' FAMOUS ENGAGEMENT WITH THE 'SERAPIS', September 23, 1779, off the Yorkshire coast**

The war on land

368   Among incidents that heightened the tension was the so-called **BOSTON MASSACRE of 1770**: 'Unhappy Boston! see thy Sons deplore Thy hallow'd Walks besmear'd with guiltless gore . . . '

367   Some years before the firing of the first shot at Lexington, indignation had been steadily mounting, increased by every appearance of the hated 'red coats'. A body of **BRITISH TROOPS QUARTERED ON BOSTON COMMON, 1768**

370 At home in Great Britain, public opinion did not minimize the seriousness of her reverses and humiliations. Witness this popular cartoon, commenting on the present-day woes of MAGNA BRITANNIA no longer mighty

369 A random shot fired at LEXINGTON on April 19, 1775—no one knows who pressed the trigger—precipitated Great Britain and her American colonies into eight years of armed conflict

XII

GEORGIAN APOGEE

The Dynasty

Very different from his grandfather, George II, and his great-grandfather, George I, those choleric and amorous German princes, was the virtuous sovereign who occupied the throne of England for sixty eventful years, between 1760 and 1820. George III was a remarkably hard-working and naturally well-meaning man; and the legend put about by his enemies and accepted by certain later historians, that he had sought deliberately to increase the power of the Crown at the expense of parliamentary rights, is nowadays believed to have had little real foundation. Unlike George I and George II, however, he had a high sense not only of his inherited dignity but of his royal duty; and to what he considered his duty he brought a somewhat limited and unstable intelligence. Nor were his advisers always well chosen. Bute, the friend and counsellor of his youth, an exceedingly unpopular politician, helped to encourage his feelings of royal self-sufficiency; North, though a master of parliamentary tactics, proved

371 George III's homely consort, **CHARLOTTE SOPHIA OF MECK-LENBURG-STRELITZ, is depicted by Zoffany (1725?-1810), the most accomplished painter-reporter of the age, at home with her children; on the right, the future George IV, in fancy dress as a Roman warrior**

372 (*below*) **In a family of prodigal sons, GEORGE IV (1820-1830) was probably the most extravagant. But during his youth he was distinguished for personal charm—there was 'fascination in his very bow'—and to the end he remained a man of genuine artistic taste**

373   From a terrace, in this portrait by Stroehling, the old King seems to be looking back across the dramas and tragedies of his lengthy reign. Born in 1738 GEORGE III ruled, with intervals of enforced retirement, from 1760 to 1820

totally incapable of confronting the larger problems of the age—among which none was so critical as the problem of the American colonies, who in 1776 severed their connection with the mother country. The King's later years were overshadowed by madness. In 1810 he became permanently insane; and his undutiful eldest son, the future George IV, assumed authority as Prince Regent.

No less lamentable than the King's public misfortunes was the tragedy of his private life. Happily married to a plain and bigoted German princess, Charlotte Sophia of Mecklenburg-Strelitz, he produced a large family of sons and daughters and set an example of solid domestic virtue. It was not an example that any of his sons followed. Their heavy debts and notorious dissipations caused their parents continual alarm and anxiety; and the heir to the throne presently threw in his lot with the forces of the opposition. Just as George II had quarrelled with George I, and Frederick Prince of Wales, George III's father, had antagonized his own father and his clever and ambitious mother, so the heir, as soon as he achieved manhood, began to shake free of parental bondage. Both in his political leanings and his private tastes, the impulsive, excitable Prince of Wales stood for everything that the old King most distrusted. During the last ten years of his life, George III, an ancient bearded recluse, was completely cut off from the ordinary world. Dead to present-day sorrows, he led a twilight life amid the visions of the past.

The Social Scene

374 Britain's prolonged struggle with France came to a victorious end in June 1815 upon the field of **WATERLOO**. But the battle had been a 'damned close-run thing', afterwards commented the Duke of Wellington. Napoleonic cavalry are seen charging an unbroken British square

Yet despite the disputes and disasters of his reign, English society under George III continued to develop and thrive. Britain asserted herself as a great colonial power, and British commerce dominated the markets of Europe; while the Revolutionary Wars and the long struggle against Napoleon Bonaparte ended at last with a decisive victory upon the field of Waterloo. In Great Britain itself, the Industrial Revolution was rapidly transforming the English rural economy; and across the landscape of the north drifted the smoke of 'black Satanic mills', built by the early industrialists to house the inventors' new machines.

Simultaneously, art and literature flourished. In the field of portrait-painting, Hogarth was succeeded by Gainsborough, Reynolds, Romney; English landscape painters began to make their mark; and the greatest of them all, Turner and Constable, were born in 1775 and 1776. But architecture and the decorative arts were probably most characteristic of the social period. If the first half of the eighteenth century may be called the age of Kent (who designed furniture as well as buildings), the second may be entitled the age of Chippendale and

375 (*opposite*) **Among the greatest glories of the Georgian apogee was its fine domestic architecture —the solid, dignified, elegantly proportioned buildings then raised by the upper and middle classes. ATTINGHAM PARK, near Shrewsbury, was built for Lord Berwick in 1785**

Robert Adam. Inspired by the ruins of antiquity which he had studied on his journeys abroad, Adam established a new school of architectural taste and gave the English upper classes a splendid background of classical magnificence. Meanwhile Chippendale produced chairs, tables and sideboards, in which classical motifs were presently enriched by the addition of Gothic and Chinese details. Never before had the Englishman's home—whether he was a member of the aristocracy or the rising middle classes—been planned on such noble and spacious lines, with so much regard for comfort, yet with so sure a sense of style. Almost as impressive as the mansions of the rich were the small houses that now began to appear in every prosperous provincial town—soberly elegant constructions of stone and brick, with finely proportioned front doors and large reception rooms, that reflected their owners' feelings for domestic ease. Above all else, it was a remarkably sociable period; and the Georgian house at its best has an extraordinarily welcoming and friendly air.

The eighteenth century was also a prosaic age, in which distinguished prose writers outnumbered poets. But before Gibbon, Johnson, Boswell and Burke had vanished from the literary scene, a new movement had begun to emerge which would soon revolutionize European literature. William Blake was born in 1757, Wordsworth in 1770, Coleridge in 1772. The spirit of Romanticism was already abroad—it had found expression in architecture as early as 1747, when Horace Walpole, a student of Gothic art, decided to build himself a little 'Gothic castle'; and the new poets broke with the classical tradition and sought their inspiration from very different sources. Like Wordsworth they were deeply moved by the revolutionary explosion in France. At the same time, they discovered a new form of literary stimulus in the contemplation of nature. The Romantic revolution swept through the world of writing. Byron became its most magnetic figure; while Keats and Shelley gave a fresh impetus to the art of English poetry—an impetus that carried it along until the death of Tennyson.

376   **The eighteenth-century Englishman was of a notably sociable and gregarious turn. Torond's lively silhouette illustrates a BIRTHDAY PARTY of the 1780s**

Plate XV (*opposite*) **Ninth son of an impover ished cloth merchant, THOMAS GAINSBOROUGH (1727-88) became one of the most fashionabl portrait painters of the age, and, as Van Dyck ha done before him, created an ideal aristocracy. Thi is his engaging portrait of 'William Poyntz'**

Statesmen

377   The friend and counsellor of George III's youth, **LORD BUTE** (1713-92) was often attacked by hostile contemporaries as a machiavellian, royal favourite. Here he instructs his secretary, later the first Lord Liverpool

378   Although loyal, good-natured, hard-working and a past-master of parliamentary tactics, **LORD NORTH** (1732-92) continued the oppressive and short-sighted policy that was ultimately to provoke the War of Independence

379   Across the floor of the House of Commons, **PITT** apostrophizes his opponent **CHARLES JAMES FOX** (1749-1806), who supported the cause of the American colonists and welcomed the outbreak of the French Revolution

380 Gainsborough's evidently somewhat idealized portrait shows the YOUNGER PITT (1759-1806) at the zenith of his life. First Prime Minister when only twenty-four, he led Great Britain in her Continental struggle

383 EDMUND BURKE (1729-97), statesman and political philosopher, like Fox had championed the American colonists; but he reacted with eloquent violence against the later revolutionary explosion in France. Portrait of Burke by George Romney

381 (below) An enlightened foreign minister, LORD CASTLEREAGH (1769-1822) became associated with a policy of repression at home that aroused the venomous hatred of English liberals. His cold, unbending, reserved character is here caught by Sir Thomas Lawrence

382 (below) When he sat for Lawrence in 1828, WILLIAM WILBERFORCE (1759-1833), politician, philanthropist and Evangelical convert, had already achieved his main parliamentary object—the triumphant passage in 1807 of a bill abolishing the infamous slave trade

384 In 1812, the architect John Nash (1752-1835) launched an ambitious scheme for the embellishment of London, linking **REGENT STREET**, named after the Prince, and the Quadrant (now Piccadilly Circus) to the magnificent pillared terraces of Regent's Park

Urban life and amusements

385 (*below*) **DUBLIN**, during the Georgian age, became one of Great Britain's most elegant cities. This watercolour by James Malton illustrates Capel Street and a bridge across the Liffey. On the left, the Lottery Office

387 (*above*) **Among the vices of the age was its passion for gambling, particularly in aristocratic circles. Thomas Rowlandson's lively talent produced this vigorous, imaginative sketch of a fashionable GAMBLING PARTY AT DEVON-SHIRE HOUSE**

386 (*below*) **Coffee houses were an important feature of the urban scene. GARRAWAY'S COFFEE HOUSE in the City of London was a favourite haunt of eighteenth-century businessmen, from which originated the modern Lloyd's**

388 **George IV's 'marine palace', known as THE ROYAL PAVILION, BRIGHTON, begun in 1784 but not completed until 1827, reflects the decline of eighteenth-century taste—a wild architectural extravaganza with aspiring minarets and bulbous Indian domes**

389 George Morland (1763-1804) as a rule was a decidedly sentimental, even a mildly mawkish, painter; but in THE ALE BENCH he shows a genuine feeling for the rough homespun background of English country life

The countryside

390 (*below*) No English artist has rendered the country pursuits of his day more brilliantly than George Stubbs (1724-1806): witness this delightful picture of THE DUKE AND DUCHESS OF RICHMOND WATCHING THEIR HORSES AT EXERCISE

391 Contentment and urbanity irradiate
the faces of the prosperous middle-aged
husband and wife whom Stubbs has im-
mortalized in THE PHAETON, behind a
well-matched pair of well-groomed horses

392 The AGRICULTURAL LABOURER, on
the other hand, might sometimes have envied the
existence of the squire's horses; and his dark
cottage often compared unfavourably with the
spacious surroundings of a good stable

High-born,

low-born

393 The celebrated courtesan **KITTY FISHER** was often painted by her friend Sir Joshua Reynolds. According to Mrs Thrale, her eyes were of a clear celestial blue, the bluest that were ever seen

394 One of the young men who left their portraits at Eton was **CHARLES GREY**, the future Lord Grey (1764-1845), sponsor of the revolutionary First Reform Bill. The artist he selected to portray him was George Romney

395 (*above*) Zoffany's conversation piece, **THE DUTTON FAMILY**, shows a domestic gathering of the eighteenth-century upper middle class. Observe the rich carpet, the fine inlaid card table and the general air of spacious comfort

396 As in Hogarth's day, the English parliamentary elections still provided fast and furious fun. This drawing was inspired by **THE WESTMINSTER ELECTION** of 1764, where the Whig leader Charles James Fox stood for the progressive party

397 **MEN O' WAR BOUND FOR THE PORT OF PLEASURE**—thus Richard Dighton represents Nelson's seamen disembarking at an English port, after many months of hard living below decks on weevily biscuits and salted meat

Poets and painters

398   The uncouth son of a country bookseller, **SAMUEL JOHNSON** (1709-84), here portrayed by James Barry, owed the great position he at length achieved to both his literary abilities and his conversational gifts

399   **SAMUEL TAYLOR COLERIDGE** (1772-1834) collaborated with Wordsworth in the production of 'Lyrical Ballads' which heralded a new poetic age, two years before the end of the eighteenth century

400   More than two thousand portraits and historical paintings received the signature of **SIR JOSHUA REYNOLDS** (1723-92). He has placed a bust of Michelangelo in the background of this self-portrait

401   Unlike the proud Sir Joshua, **GAINSBOROUGH**, we are told, had 'little taste for the high society he painted'. He is at his happiest in this charming early group of **THE ARTIST AND HIS FAMILY**

402   The early death of **JOHN KEATS** (1795-1821) deprived the English Romantic Movement of one of its proudest and most gifted spirits. His friend Joseph Severn shows him reading in his Hampstead study

403   While Keats died too young, **WILLIAM WORDSWORTH** (1770-1850) had the misfortune to outlive his genius. 'The Prelude', his luminous poetic autobiography, was completed as early as 1805

Plate XVI **From Old Northumberland House, near Charing Cross, comes this sumptuous DOORWAY DESIGNED BY ROBERT ADAM, carried out with the intricate classical details and in the glowing colours that the Scottish master loved. As at Syon House, his client was the Duke of Northumberland**

404 (*below*) **ROBERT ADAM** (1728-92) had originally derived his inspiration from a visit to the ruins of Diocletian's palace in Dalmatia, on which he published a famous book in 1764. Among his greatest triumphs was the decoration of **SYON HOUSE** near London, 405 (*right*)—an edifice capable of 'holding its own with the lesser palaces of the Continent'—of which a chimney-piece is shown here

'COUNTRY LIFE'

An age of elegance

406 (*below*) **Many of the eighteenth century's pleasantest buildings were planned on a comparatively modest scale: for example, this elegant row of unpretentious stone-built houses at SION HILL PLACE, BATH**

Sailor and soldier

407 (*above*) **Petty, vainglorious, childish, yet full of an 'infinite fire' as the commander of a fleet, HORATIO NELSON (1758-1805) is here depicted in his early manhood. On the eve of Trafalgar, his last engagement, which finally swept away fears of a French invasion, he scrawled this moving FAREWELL LETTER,** 408 (*right*), **to his beloved Lady Hamilton**

Victory Octr: 19: 1805
Noon Cadiz ESE 16 Leagues

My Dearest beloved Emma the dear friend of my bosom the Signal has been made that the Enemys Combined fleet are coming out of Port, We have very little Wind so that I have no hopes of seeing them before to morrow may the God of Battles crown my Endeavours with success at all events I will take care that my name shall ever be most dear to You and Horatia both of whom I love as much as my own life, and as my last writing before the battle will be to You so I hope in God that I shall live to finish my letter after th

409 (*above*) **Beside his camp-fire in the Pyrenees, in July 1813, WELLINGTON** (1769-1852) **looks forward to his victorious invasion of France, at the close of the long campaign in which he drove the French army from the Spanish Peninsula.** 410 (*below*) **Chelsea pensioners, outside their ancient Hospital, celebrate the NEWS OF WATERLOO: a picture by Sir David Wilkie**

The Industrial Revolution

411   During the closing decades of the period, science and industry made prodigious strides. **SIR HUMPHREY DAVY** (1778-1829), chemist and inventor of a safety lamp for miners, was a gifted representative of the new scientific class

412 (*below*) Meanwhile the Industrial Revolution had begun to transform the English landscape. As in Loutherbourg's picture of **THE IRON WORKS AT COALBROOKDALE**, its strongholds were often invested by artists with an air of lurid splendour

413   The Industrial age found its own painter in the gifted and versatile Joseph Wright of Derby (1734-97), whose darkly dramatic impression of THE IRON FORGE illustrates the rough-and-ready methods of the time

414   (*below*) Two little girls brought in to admire an EXPERIMENT WITH AN AIR-PUMP shrink from the spectacle of the bird being slowly suffocated. Another romantic canvas by Joseph Wright, whose paintings show the pleasure he took in reflected light

XIII

THE NEW REPUBLIC

The Union Constituted

A most precarious future seemed to confront the thirteen states at the end of the War of Independence. Associated together by only the loosest of bonds, they were moved by widely divergent hopes and interests, burdened by debt and inflation, and distracted by disputes with Britain unresolved in the Peace Treaty. Visitors from Europe in those early days, failing to grasp the self-confidence of the mass of Americans, or the spirit of practical energy on which it was grounded, nearly all forecast an anarchic future for the new nation. Yet within the span of an adult's lifetime, Tocqueville was to hold up the achievements of *Democracy in America* to European admiration. It is not surprising that a robust belief in progress has ever since inspired the outlook of Americans; for their own national progress during the decades after 1783 was swift, sure-footed and astonishing.

The initial step in the summer of 1787 was the drafting of the oldest written Constitution in the modern world. Amid the tug of conflicting principles, and after many hesitations, the document that was to form the basis of American institutions was ratified by all the states. Meanwhile, a Congress was elected; Washington was inaugurated as President in New York, a Federal administration was appointed and the Supreme Court came into being. The instruments of government were now all at hand for the realization of American unity. *E Pluribus*

415 THE PRESIDENT'S HOUSE, Washington, as it appeared in 1831; reconstructed after being burnt by the British in 1814, the smoke-stained walls were painted white, a colour that gave the building its modern name

416 On the eve of his retirement in 1796, the first President of the United States issued his Farewell Address, in which he warned the nation of the dangers of party strife and laid down the principles of its foreign policy. WASHINGTON IN OLD AGE, after A. de Saint-Memin

417 An idealist in politics, who exercised an imposing variety of practical gifts, THOMAS JEFFERSON (1743-1826), the third President, was one of the prime founders of the American democratic tradition. A painting by R. Peale

unum was the new Federal motto; and it is the distinction of Washington and his immediate successors in office that they converted this aspiration into a fact. The tradition they created was strong enough seventy years later to withstand secession, and to sustain the cause of the North throughout the great testing time of the Union.

A week after Washington took office, the French States-General met at Versailles, and a revolutionary course of events began that led to a generation of European warfare. Out of this turmoil, important repercussions spread to the United States. American sympathies were divided between France and Britain; and this cleavage whetted the numerous domestic differences of opinion, out of which the two-party habit in political life, under varying names, was gradually growing. More significant for the future, Napoleon Bonaparte's preoccupations induced him to sell to President Jefferson in 1803 the immense territories named Louisiana which he had acquired from Spain. For less than twelve million dollars, the lands between the Mississippi and the Rocky Mountains passed into American possession. There was now no hindrance to westward expansion towards the Pacific Ocean; and in the years 1803–6, Captains Lewis and Clark, on Jefferson's orders, blazed the trail from St. Louis to the mouth of the Columbia River.

418 **The United States negotiators, Robert R. Livingston and James Monroe on May 2, 1803, signed the treaty with Napoleon's ministers by which the vast French territories of THE LOUISIANA PURCHASE came under the American flag. A lithograph after a painting by Victor Adam**

Meanwhile, the world struggle at sea, and the British blockade of France, were giving rise to frequent Anglo-American disputes that eventually exploded into the War of 1812. The irritations that caused this outbreak were not beyond compounding; and, with a few glorious exceptions, the conduct of hostilities was scarcely distinguished. Even Andrew Jackson's striking victory at New Orleans was gained unnecessarily, after peace had been signed, but before the news could cross the Atlantic. Although, on the American side, the war had been unpopular in many states, especially in New England, it nevertheless had lasting effects on the continental scene. To United States thinking, it came to be regarded as a second War of Independence that had served to consolidate the sense of American identity. The Battle of New Orleans became a landmark in history books comparable to Saratoga and Yorktown. On the practical plane, however, the war had disappointing results for American patriots: it put an end to their dreams of incorporating Canada into the Union. Henceforth the northern provinces of the continent were to work out their own separate sphere of dominion.

Many people on both shores of the Atlantic, in the years after Waterloo, considered a third Anglo-American war to be inevitable.

419 **Politics in George Caleb Bingham's picture is a function in which the whole community shares; his election scene, THE VERDICT OF THE PEOPLE, was painted in 1855**

Their forbodings went happily unfulfilled; and the festering boundary dispute with Canada was finally settled by the Oregon Treaty of 1846. Peace now reigned over the three thousand miles of frontier. Two wars had generated feelings of respect between the two main branches of English-speaking peoples, as well as an open acknowledgment of differences. A forbearance of these, and a certain mutual affection, took much longer to grow and required, for its sealing, fellowship in arms in twentieth-century wars. But, meanwhile, revolution in Latin America had provoked the first demonstration of common interests between the United States and Britain. Independence for the former Spanish colonies and for Brazil lay to British, as well as to American, advantage. President Monroe's doctrine, directed against European intervention on the continent, was not entirely welcome to George Canning in London—who saw in it a United States pretension to put themselves at the head of a confederacy of the Americas. But Britain had the wisdom to acquiesce.

The Moving Frontier   One of the far-sighted decisions of the Founding Fathers had been to allow for the admission of new states to the Union, formed from the territories of the West. As the continent began to fill, and the Indian

Plate XVII   **A tobacco port, centre of shipbuilding, starting point of railroads to the west, the CITY OF BALTIMORE** grew rapidly in importance; lithograph of 1848, after A. Kollner

tribes were displaced amid struggles commemorated by American novelists and historians, the territories of the Mississippi valley one after another rose to statehood. The American frontier was moving West. Texas broke free from Mexico and, ten years later, joined the Union. California followed suit, and the other territories of the South-West were gained in 1848 as a result of the war with Mexico. By mid-century the United States stretched from ocean to ocean, and its population, which had counted about five million in 1800, had increased five times over, and now outnumbered the peoples of the British isles.

While the Westward movement was shaping the American future, the intellectual capitals of the country on the Eastern seaboard were steadily growing in stature and diversity. In New England a literary and moral tradition flowered in the works of Emerson, Hawthorne, Thoreau and Longfellow, and history found its first American masters in Bancroft, Prescott, Motley and Parkman. From New York, the unique voice of Whitman and the powerful genius of Melville were slower to gain their countrymen's attention; but for them the passage of time enlarged their distinctive American look. Soon, to these developments was to be added the individual blend of myth and humour characteristic of the West. Thus, as the states multiplied, they generated their own cultural climate that was at once different from the European model, yet constantly interacting with it.

The rise of the West added new sectional interests to American politics that henceforth had to be balanced against those of the old Atlantic colonies. Virginia and Massachusetts had supplied the first six presidents; but in 1828 the West arrived in the White House in the person of General Andrew Jackson. Frontier democracy enjoyed its first triumph over the landed and mercantile aristocracy of the East. The Great Divide, in American history, however, was to be marked by a parallel, not a longitude. Two surveyors in colonial times, Mason and Dixon, had drawn a boundary between Pennsylvania and Maryland that lent its name to the broadening cleavage. While the country was physically becoming ever more closely linked by canals, turnpikes, steamboats and railroads, it was splitting on a matter of principle, into North and South. Slavery was the issue, crystallized in the problem of whether it should be extended to the new territories of the West. From 1820 onwards, numerous compromises were attempted, but none endured. For beneath the principle at stake lay the growing conviction of the Southern states that they were in danger of being overwhelmed by the North and outstripped in the race for the West.

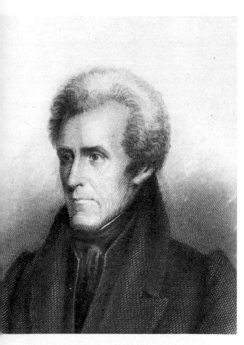

20 The victor of New Orleans in January 1815, man of action and champion of the West, General ANDREW JACKSON (1767-1845) as seventh President brought to the White House a popular, reforming, egalitarian spirit

Men of State

421 Washington's aide-de-camp and Secretary of the Treasury under his presidency, **ALEXANDER HAMILTON** (1757-1804) played a leading part in the making of the Constitution and in the establishment of the central organs of administration

422 After a distinguished diplomatic career in Europe, **JOHN QUINCY ADAMS** (1767-1848) as Secretary of State in 1823 formulated the Doctrine that goes by President Monroe's name; his own presidency in 1824-28 was less happy

423 A leading federalist, Secretary of State under Jefferson and his successor at the White House, JAMES MADISON (1751-1836) conducted the unhappy war of 1812 with Britain. A painting of the President by Mrs Sharples

424 A highly successful attorney and most eloquent orator, DANIEL WEBSTER (1782-1852), defended the cause of Union in the Senate amid the rising tides of sectionalism; he was three times Secretary of State

425 Spokesman for the planters' aristocracy of the South and exponent of states' rights, JOHN C. CALHOUN (1782-1850) helped to lay the political foundations on which the Confederacy was reared

Life in

the towns

426 In the hush of snowbound Broadway, on January 12, 1841, this party of musical New Yorkers, top-hatted and frock-coated, assembled to perform A SERENADE—intended presumably for the mysterious figure silhouetted against a lighted window. Drawing from an album by an unknown artist

427 In comparison with the cosmopolitan excitement of New York, the 'Athens of America' preserved its soberly traditional air. This view of TREMONT STREET, BOSTON, about 1820, is strongly suggestive of an English country town of the same period

428 The completion of the Erie Canal in 1825 had immensely hastened New York's growth, as immigrants flowed in from Europe and natural produce from the West. In 1848, over three thousand vessels landed nearly 180,000 people. NEW YORK DURING THE EIGHTEEN-FIFTIES

429 Founded in 1682 by the intrepid Quaker colonist William Penn, the 'City of Brotherly Love' developed as one of the main strongholds of the new American civilization. PHILADELPHIA FROM THE GREAT TREE, KENSINGTON, 1812

Country

Life

430   **HARNESS RACING IN 1850. Before the American Revolution, racing was already popular. After the introduction of the sulky during the eighteen-thirties, vehicle-pulling events began to be held on many American racecourses. Picture of a contestant by an unknown artist**

431   **Very often the untutored artist showed a rare degree of calligraphic skill. This picture by Leila T. Bauman of WILD GEESE IN FLIGHT, which was painted about 1860, bears a curious and interesting resemblance to the work of some early Chinese masters**

432 The American artist was rapidly awaking to the romantic interest of his native landscape; which he no longer attempted to portray in imagery borrowed from European art. THE GENESSEE FALLS AT ROCHESTER, N.Y., by Thomas Chambers

433 George Caleb Bingham (1811-79) was a romantic genre painter, who extended his artistic operations from his home in Missouri to Mississippi and the South, where he executed this typical canvas entitled RAFTSMEN PLAYING CARDS

434 (*below*) American artists of the mid-nineteenth century, like contemporary English painters, excelled at cosily anecdotal scenes, brightened by domestic sentiment—such as this lively representation of a FAMILY PICNIC AT THE SEASIDE by an unknown painter

The frontier

435   Frontiersman and famous Indian-fighter, DAVID CROCKETT (1786-1836) has earned himself a secure place in American folk-mythology. He lost his life at the BATTLE OF THE ALAMO, fought against the Mexican rulers of Texas; a drawing in 1834

436   OSCEOLA, chief of the Seminoles, established in Florida since the early eighteenth century, who was finally subjugated in 1842, at the cost of the most expensive Indian war ever fought by the United States

438 The poisons of modern civilization soon corrupted the primitive Indian economy. WI-JUN-JON, an Assiniboin chief, (*left*) arriving to hold conference at Washington and (*right*) departing; engraved by George Catlin, 1844

439 (*above*) The western frontier produced its legendary heroes, among whom none was more celebrated than Daniel Boone, explorer, settler, frontier-fighter (1734-1820). **DANIEL BOONE COMING THROUGH CUMBERLAND GAP**, painted by George Caleb Bingham in 1851

440 (*below*) On **BUFFALO HUNTING** the Indians of the plains had long depended for their means of life. They were soon joined by professional hide-hunters and frontier marksmen working for construction camps, until the vast nomadic herds had been entirely wiped out

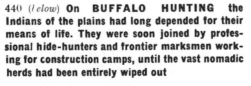

437 (*left*) **MATO-TOPE**, a Mandan chief, whose tribe ranged the territories of North Dakota, was drawn in 1840 by Carl Bodmer, to illustrate the travel-book of an itinerant German prince

Men of letters and learning

441 (*above*) **POE'S COTTAGE AT FORDHAM**, now a museum, became his precarious refuge in 1846, a year before his wife's death. Here he wrote his review of the literary scene entitled 'The Literati of New York City'

442 (*right*) **The varied but fragmentary genius of EDGAR ALLAN POE** (1809-49) exerted a profound influence on nineteenth-century European writers particularly on such French poets as Charles Baudelaire and Stephane Mallarmé

443 Despite his deep regard for the civilization of the Old World, RALPH WALDO EMERSON (1803-82) summoned his own country to proclaim its cultural independence and build a new literature that should be distinctively American; in this he was a pioneer

444 The national recognition that had eluded Poe was awarded, in full measure, to HENRY WADSWORTH LONGFELLOW (1807-82). This impressive portrait is the work of a famous English photographer, Julia Margaret Cameron

445 (left) What, as an earnest Northerner, she had seen of fugitive slaves and heard of conditions in the South inspired Harriet Beecher Stowe (1811-96) to produce in 1851 'Uncle Tom's Cabin', one of the most effective of all propagandist novels. UNCLE TOM AND LITTLE EVA

American men and women

446 & 447   Before the daguerreotype, and other forms of photography, reached America, portrait painters were much in demand among prosperous households to record the features of their presiding ladies. Mrs ELIZA STONE WELCH, in about 1835, (446 *left*) is an imposing matron with ringlets; a YOUNG WOMAN (447 *above*), with elaborate lace collar, fondles her lapdog

227

448 Depicted in 1837 by Isaac Sheffield at the age of five years and ten months, JAMES FRANCIS SMITH, wearing a coat made of penguin skins, disembarks in Connecticut after a voyage from the South Seas, where American enterprise was active

449 The itinerant artist, Joseph H. Davis, who signed himself 'Left-hand painter', specialized in profiles of husbands and wives calmly confronting one another against their staid domestic background. Joint portrait of MR AND MRS JOSEPH EMERY, 1834

450 MRS BRADLEY OF CATSKILL, New York, wearing an attractive lace cap, was painted by an artist named Phillips in 1832, the year of President Jackson's re-election

228

American Houses

451 (*right*) **Thomas Jefferson himself designed the graceful house on his estate of MONTICELLO, near Charlottesville, Virginia; he moved into the part-built mansion in 1772 and lived there for more than fifty years**

452 (*below*) **Washington's home overlooking the Potomac is now a national shrine; the mansion has been restored in accordance with the President's detailed notes of his possessions; a rear view of MOUNT VERNON today**

453 Longfellow's home, CRAIGIE HOUSE, Cambridge, Massachusetts, became a centre of literary pilgrimage during the poet's long life and distinguished professorship at Harvard

454 French influence in NEW ORLEANS is commemorated by the graceful architecture of the city; this elaborately wrought-iron balcony recalls the tastes and glories of an earlier civilization

455 The **YOUNG QUEEN**; a medallion designed by Henry Weigall and issued in the year of her accession

XIV

THE VICTORIAN AGE

Victoria Regina

When, on June 20, 1837, King William IV died and was succeeded by his eighteen-year-old niece, the immediate effect that the young Queen produced was captivating, even dazzling. Courtiers and politicians alike marvelled at her extraordinary combination of natural charm and regal dignity; and not until 1839, when her obstinacy and wilfulness provoked a serious cabinet crisis, did it become apparent that the sovereign's character under that pleasing surface concealed a vein of iron. But in Prince Albert, whom she presently agreed to marry —as a reigning monarch, she had herself to propose—she found a companion whose will-power matched her own. During their marriage, which ran its fruitful and harmonious course from 1840 to 1861, the Prince—created Prince Consort in 1857—established a position of unique authority. Had he lived longer, the history of the British monarchy might perhaps have taken a very different course.

The death of the husband she adored dealt the Queen a crushing personal blow. During the years of neurotic seclusion that followed, when she could seldom be persuaded to make a public appearance and never consented to discard the uniform of grief, her popularity, once so high, declined to a very low level. But the inconsolable 'Widow of Windsor' was gradually induced to reassume her royal functions; and here the influence of Benjamin Disraeli, with his unequalled blend of statesmanship and showmanship—a parliamentary leader whom the

Plate XVIII Except for Queen Elizabeth I, no English sovereign has been more closely identified with an historic age than QUEEN VICTORIA (1837-1901); both her virtues and her limitations reflected the moral spirit of the nation over which she presided. Portrait by Winterhalter

456 The royal family happily exempli-fied the domestic virtues; a group painted at Windsor by Sir Edwin Landseer (1802-73) of THE QUEEN, PRINCE ALBERT, the baby Princess Royal, dogs and game

The emergence of Modern England

Queen appreciated as much as she disliked and distrusted his rival Gladstone—played a happy and beneficent part. By 1887, the fiftieth anniversary of her accession, Queen Victoria had become the living symbol of the vast empire over which she ruled. Ten years later, her Diamond Jubilee was celebrated in a blaze of triumph. An almost legendary figure, the royal matriarch of Europe, she died on January 22, 1901.

The age to which Victoria gave her name witnessed the creation of modern England. It saw the rapid rise of the middle class, who had begun to make themselves felt as a parliamentary power since the passage of the First Reform Bill under the reign of her uncle William IV in the year 1832. During the 'forties, a wave of revolutionary unrest seemed to threaten the established social system. But in 1848, while popular revolts were shaking so many European thrones, the English Chartists were content to prepare a monster petition; after which Chartism rapidly dwindled into insignificance. A new spirit possessed the community at large, epitomized in such manuals as Samuel Smiles' *Self-Help*. Inspired by the example of the Court itself—now the proto-type of a happy middle-class home—a cult of domestic virtue replaced the comparative laxity of Georgian manners; and with respectability went a tremendous access of national prosperity. Earlier than any of her European neighbours, Great Britain reaped the benefits of the Industrial Revolution. But this revolution also brought its problems.

457 **Thousands of acres of London were covered with TERRACED WORKING-CLASS HOUSES,** huddled amid the arched viaducts of the grimy railway age; an engraving by the Romantic French artist, Gustave Doré, 1876

The gospel of the Victorian businessman was that of the so-called 'Manchester School'—economists who preached the doctrine of commercial *laissez faire*, which presupposed the existence of 'natural laws' regulating the supply of labour. Poverty and unemployment, they implied, were a natural consequence of growing wealth: the industrialists, who enriched the nation, were entitled to procure labour at the lowest wages they could persuade the labourer to accept. Otherwise the flow of wealth, which would at length abolish poverty, might be dammed up before it had had time time to circulate. When Ruskin protested against their theory, in his courageous volume *Unto This Last*, his protests were denounced by the London *Times* as the ravings of a 'mad governess'. The misery and degradation of the English industrial towns continued to appal the foreign visitor.

Simultaneously, visitors were astonished to observe that respectability and prosperity existed cheek by jowl with vice and crime. London swarmed with prostitutes; and organized commercial vice had a monopoly of many London streets, including the Haymarket just off Piccadilly, where night-houses and other raffish results 'literally blazed with light' from dusk until dawn. The criminal population was large; and in some regions of the metropolis, for example Seven Dials, no ordinary pedestrian liked to venture and a policeman dared not walk alone. Victorian philanthropists were numerous and active; but the immensity of the problem defied their efforts. Nineteenth-century Lon-

458 **In 1854 the CRYSTAL PALACE,** built of glass and iron by a master of conservatory design, Sir Joseph Paxton (1801-65), was re-erected at Sydenham, Surrey, and survived as a showpiece until its destruction by fire in 1936

don was a pattern of violently contrasted scenes—aristocratic splendour and middle-class comfort, displayed in the squares of Mayfair and Belgravia and the streets of the rapidly expanding suburbs, were set off by the darkness and squalor of proletarian slum districts.

Art, Literature and Thought

Meanwhile, taste had declined as industrial civilization overwhelmed the artist; and the Great Exhibition of 1851, when Paxton's Crystal Palace became a glittering show-case for the nation's manufactured goods, showed how disastrously artistic standards had degenerated since the beginning of the century. William Morris and his pre-Raphaelite allies, shocked by the ugliness of everyday English life, were soon to set about a reformation; but, as a general rule, the Victorian Englishman, whose eighteenth-century ancestors had patronized Chippendale and Adam, showed comparatively little interest in the development of the visual arts.

Literature, on the other hand, never ceased to flourish. Besides popular novelists like Dickens, Thackeray and Trollope, England produced a long series of influential literary prophets—Carlyle, with his doctrine of work: Ruskin, art critic and social reformer, constantly at war against the crude materialism of his times: Matthew Arnold, poet-prophet, striving to bring traditional faith into line with nineteenth-century requirements: Morris, a founder of modern Socialism, who derived his inspiration from an imaginative vision of the Middle Ages. Meanwhile Tennyson, last of the Romantics, lent dignity to the

459 **The present HOUSES OF PAR-LIAMENT** at Westminster are the work of Sir Charles Barry (1795-1860); the roofs of the Gothic building, with the Thames in the background, seen from the Victoria Tower

Poet Laureate's role. The British reading public was immense and receptive—far more receptive, indeed, than the reading public of the present day.

Among the various important issues that exercised thoughtful and well-educated Victorian minds, none was discussed with greater eagerness—at times with greater acrimony—than the clash between faith and modern science. By presuming to cast doubts on the literal accuracy of the first five books of the Old Testament, Bishop Colenso horrified orthodox churchmen and alarmed even such unorthodox thinkers as Matthew Arnold; while the publication in 1859 of Charles Darwin's *Origin of Species* aroused a storm of public controversy that, despite the valiant support of T. H. Huxley, continued to rage for many years. But there was nothing Voltairian about English free-thinkers: in that formidable scholar John Stuart Mill, nineteenth-century rationalism had its own saint.

Often described, the weaknesses of the Victorian character have sometimes been exaggerated. The period that produced it was an age of high seriousness, not necessarily to be confused with smugness—of idealism that did not preclude cynicism, but was founded, in the last resort, upon a passionate sense of right and wrong. Thus Gladstone owed his political ascendancy to his hold upon his hearers' conscience. He invited them, we are told, 'to join with him in a moral judgment, to leave their own problems where they belonged . . . and to share with him the duties imposed by membership of a great and free nation'. Such

460 **Four times Prime Minister of Britain, WILLIAM EWART GLAD-STONE** (1809-98), leader of the Liberal party, master of eloquence, in whom the highest moral principles were equally blended with astute political calculation; reading in his library at Hawarden

an attitude usually comes to the fore in a period of prosperity and peace; and, from the accession of Queen Victoria to the closing years of her singularly untroubled reign, only two major conflicts—the Crimean War, which broke out in 1854, and the Indian Mutiny of 1857 and 1858—tried the morale of the British people. Naturally, as the British Empire expanded, minor conflicts occurred and blood was shed; but these clashes were accepted as part of the price that must be paid for ruling; and such battles were always fought by small dedicated professional armies. Not until the disasters of the Boer War did it occur to the average nineteenth-century Englishman, either that English strength would not eventually prevail, or that it might possibly be exerted in an unjust cause. He had more than sixty years of continuous progress behind him: he felt justifiably proud of his solid achievement since the accession of his venerable Queen. But the South African struggle shook his complacency; and he crossed the threshold of the twentieth century in a somewhat chastened and disillusioned mood.

461 **To his sovereign's gratification, the deviser of the Indian Empire, BENJAMIN DISRAELI** (1804-81), Earl of Beaconsfield, Conservative Prime Minister and an arbiter of European destiny at the Congress of Berlin in 1878

462   **THE QUEEN** riding at Windsor with her
first Prime Minister, in grey top hat; William
Lamb, **LORD MELBOURNE** (1779-1848), leader
of the Whigs, was his young sovereign's affection-
ate and worldly-wise preceptor in statecraft

463   During the early years of her reign, the **DUKE
OF WELLINGTON** (1769-1852) played the part of
conservative Elder Statesman; while **SIR ROBERT
PEEL** (1788-1850), whom she had first disliked,
gradually gained the Queen's confidence

The Queen

and

her statesmen

464 **THE ROYAL MATRIARCH,** Queen Victoria at the age of seventy-five. From a long period of inconsolable retirement the Queen emerged as an almost legendary figure. Towards the end of her reign only her oldest subjects could remember any other British sovereign

465 Throughout the whole reign, the Irish question continued to bedevil British politics. **CHARLES STEWART PARNELL** (1846-91) was the champion of the Irish cause in Parliament from 1875 until his tragic fall in 1890

466 **THE MARQUESS OF SALISBURY** (1830-1903), aristocratic descendant of Queen Elizabeth's famous secretary; thrice Prime Minister, and for a period of fifty years a shrewd and cautious exponent of British conservative policies both at home and abroad

The Empire

467   GENERAL SIR GEORGE BROWN fought under Wellington in Spain and against America in 1814; he led the Light Division in the war with Russia. Photograph of the veteran commander with members of his personal staff in the Crimea, 1855

468   The Crimean war centred in the siege of Sebastopol; one of the Russ fortresses, the REDAN, was long assaulted in vain by British troops. Pho graph of the interior after the Russian withdrawal, 1855

469   The dethronement of the King of Oudh helped to precipitate the Indian Mutiny. At Lucknow in Oudh a small British garrison held out against a Sepoy army. RUINS OF THE BRITISH RESIDENCY, 1858

470   During the Sepoy Rebellion in India, some of the heaviest fighting took place around Delhi, the ancient Mogul capital. A BRITISH BATTERY in action during the siege of the city, 1857

471 Difficulties with Egypt and a threat to the Suez Canal led to Gladstone's decision to intervene with arms. A British BLUEJACKET ON GUARD IN ALEXANDRIA, after the capture of the city, August 1882

472 The advance of the Empire in 1885 was marked by the annexation of Upper Burma and the DEPOSITION OF KING THEBAW, who had alarmed the British authorities by intriguing with the emissaries of France

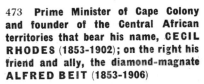

473 Prime Minister of Cape Colony and founder of the Central African territories that bear his name, CECIL RHODES (1853-1902); on the right his friend and ally, the diamond-magnate ALFRED BEIT (1853-1906)

474 The South African War began with a series of notable successes for the Boer Republics; the British fix bayonets in the TRENCHES BEFORE LADYSMITH, Natal, during the siege of the town

Eminent Victorians

475 (*opposite*) **While Africa was still the 'Dark Continent', DAVID LIVINGSTONE (1813-73), devoted missionary and intrepid explorer, helped to open up enormous tracts of territory, inspired by his determination to stamp out the slave trade**

476 **No opposition, domestic or official, could daunt the obstinate courage and fierce energy of FLORENCE NIGHTINGALE (1820-1910) whose heroic efforts in the pestiferous hospitals of the Crimea revolutionized contemporary ideas of hygiene. Portrait by Richmond, 1884**

477 (*below*) **Like his friend Carlyle, JOHN RUSKIN (1819-1900), a brilliant art-critic who during middle age turned passionate social reformer, saw much to fear and little to hope in the development of the nineteenth-century world. Portrait in 1853 by John Millais (1829-96)**

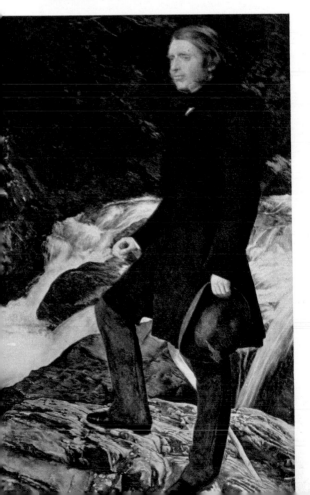

478 **Here the 'Saint of Rationalism', JOHN STUART MILL (1806-73), author of 'Principles of Political Economy', is shown by a caricaturist in 'Punch' preparing to brush aside John Bull as he leads his personal crusade for the rights of the unenfranchised sex**

Writers and thinkers

480 (*right*) **The immensely prolific genius of CHARLES DICKENS (1812-70) began to appear during the early eighteen-thirties. In 1850 he published 'David Copperfield', the novel that he himself preferred. Dickens in later life with his daughters**

479 **Women novelists such as GEORGE ELIOT, born Mary Ann Evans (1819-80), now felt themselves competent to undertake the most far-reaching social, moral and philosophical questions. Her masterpiece, 'Middlemarch', was published in 1871-2. Portrait by Sir Frederick Burton**

481 Although the early poems of ALFRED TENNYSON (1809-92) breathe a spirit of deep romantic pessimism, by 1845, when he received a government pension, he was already taking an honoured place among Victorian great men. The laureateship and a British peerage followed

482 In an age that produced many prophets, none spoke with a more powerful—at times, with a more embittered and cantankerous—voice than THOMAS CARLYLE (1795-1881), arch-opponent of all the more specious hopes based on parliamentary democracy. Portrait by Whistler

483 THOMAS BABINGTON MACAULAY (1800-59), historian, essayist and distinguished public servant, carried on the great historical tradition founded in the eighteenth century by Gibbon, while presenting the British past from the point of view of an enlightened Liberal thinker

484 HERBERT SPENCER (1820-1903) applied the evolutionary principle, as Darwin had outlined it in the study of biology, to many different fields of human knowledge. Cartoon of the austere philosopher in 'Vanity Fair'

Working,

living,

arguing

485   Dickens had attacked the London slums; but some of the worst districts remained almost untouched to the end of the nineteenth century. AN OLD CLOTHES SHOP in Seven Dials, one of the populous criminal neighbourhoods where Victorian policemen seldom walked alone

486   In 1825, the first railway passenger service was opened on the Stockton-Darlington line; and by the 'forties ambitious British promoters had launched a speculative 'railway mania'. DRAINING A TUNNEL on the London & Birmingham Railway, 1839

487   During 1848, most of Europe was ablaze with revolutionary fires. Meanwhile the CHARTISTS of Great Britain organized a peaceful procession to Westminster, carrying a monster petition in which they appealed for parliamentary aid. Chartist Demonstration on the march

490 (*below*)   Over the granite cobblestones of London's streets rumbled the heavy horse-omnibus. Inside passengers sat with their feet in damp straw, while outside passengers clung to the narrow slippery roof. DRIVER AND CONDUCTOR OF A LONDON BUS

489   CHARING CROSS about 1880. Behind, and to the left of, King Charles's statue stands the Jacobean facade of old Northumberland House, demolished not long afterwards, a nobleman's London house decorated within by Robert Adam

488   One of the most successful Victorian engineers was Isambard Kingdom Brunel (1806-59) whose great achievement, THE ALBERT VIADUCT AT SALTASH, was opened by the Prince Consort shortly before its author's death

491   In the new factories Victorian manufacturers, inspired by the 'laissez faire' doctrines of the Manchester School, felt entitled to employ labour at the lowest wages their labourers would accept. Women and children tending the machines in a COTTON MILL, 1842

492 (*opposite*)   The POPULAR PRESS was both sensational and richly illustrated. Not until the late 'eighties did Alfred Harmsworth, afterwards Lord Northcliffe, produce a more respectable form of popular journalism. The Tragedy of Todmorden Parsonage from a penny paper of 1868

THE PENNY
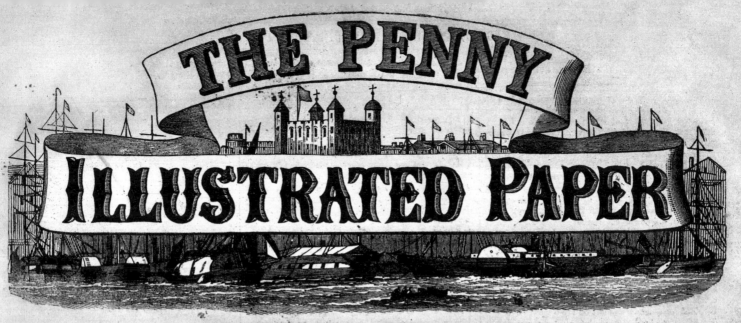
ILLUSTRATED PAPER

REGISTERED AT THE GENERAL POST OFFICE FOR TRANSMISSION ABROAD.

No. 337.   LONDON, SATURDAY, MARCH 14, 1868.   Vol. XIV.

493   The Prince of Wales bore less resemblance to his chaste and upright father than to his pleasure-loving Hanoverian great-uncles. His unruly character puzzled and disturbed his parents. Wedding picture of the PRINCE OF WALES AND PRINCESS ALEXANDRA OF DENMARK, March 10, 1863

The royal influence

494   The death of the Prince Consort—who was not only an adored husband but her permanent secretary and chief adviser —left Queen Victoria inconsolable. Photograph by her son, Prince Alfred, of THE WIDOWED QUEEN AND PRINCESS ALICE paying tribute to the Prince Consort's bust

Plate XIX   The Great Exhibition of 18 sponsored by Prince Albert, displayed the world the progress of British achie ment in the mid-nineteenth century; magnificent CRYSTAL PALACE, erec in Hyde Park, attracted over a mill visitors a month

FROM CIVIL WAR TO WORLD POWER

On November 6, 1860, Abraham Lincoln, the gaunt, homely, eloquent lawyer from Springfield, Ilinois, was elected President of the United States. Like Oliver Cromwell before him and Winston Churchill after him, Lincoln possessed an unequalled gift of fixing great issues in simple but resounding language. Already he had voiced his firm belief that a house divided against itself could not stand, that 'this government cannot endure permanently half slave and half free'; and his election almost immediately brought to a head a problem that had long been threatening the Union. The movement for the abolition of slavery was as old as the beginnings of the Republic; even during the War of Independence it had had its advocates; but, in the course of time, the 'peculiar institution' had become so necessary a part of Southern economic life that, at least among those who reaped its benefits, it had gradually 'ceased to appear evil'. Yet not all its opponents were Northerners; they included, for example, a Virginian colonel, named Robert E. Lee, then serving on the south-western frontier, who wrote that slavery is a 'moral and political evil' whatever its reasons and wherever it existed. When the break occurred, many opponents of slavery found their way into the Southern ranks. For another principle determined them—the doctrine of states' rights, that had already caused tensions within the Union over tariffs and allied financial questions and has not ceased to stir political opinions today. According to their view of the Constitution, the Southern states felt that they could legitimately nullify any federal ruling that ran contrary to their policies. On these grounds, many men deliberately chose to set the interests of their states above those of the Union, and took up arms

496 **The commander of the South, whose army 'carried the Confederacy on its bayonets', GENERAL ROBERT E. LEE poses with his son and a member of his staff in 1865 on the porch of his house in Richmond, Virginia**

495 **'The Union of these States is perpetual', said ABRAHAM LINCOLN (1809-65); by magnificent leadership during the Civil War the President successfully upheld 'the form and substance of government whose leading object is to elevate the condition of man'. Photograph by Rice**

against the economic power of the North and against a Union imposed upon them by what they considered an oppressive central government.

The Civil War

Southern Carolina's Ordinance of Secession was proclaimed in December 1860; other Southern states soon followed suit; Jefferson Davis was chosen President of a new confederacy; and, a small detachment of Federal troops having been cut off at Fort Sumter, Lincoln, in April 1861, gave orders for revictualling the beleaguered outpost. The South replied by bombardment; and, early on the twelfth of that month, Confederate artillery opened fire.

In the four-year struggle that followed, all the resources that could be mobilized on either side were thrown into combat. The North held the advantage in industry, shipping and wealth; the South had little but the cotton crop, on which were built vain hopes of recognition and support from its European customers. But, if the South was materially poor, its defensive position was strong; it attracted the loyalty of many of the ablest senior army officers, and its forces were inspired by a formidable fighting spirit. The North had all the power to win; but it needed Lincoln's indomitable genius to organize its victory.

From the bombardment of Fort Sumter to the last tragic scene of the conflict in April 1865, when General Lee rode to Appomattox Court-house to seek terms for the Army of Northern Virginia—he received them with the magnanimous addition that his men might keep their horses and mules, which they were likely to need during the spring ploughing—the American Civil War provided a spectacle that fascinated and horrified every country of the world. In Lee himself—described by Sir Winston Churchill as 'one of the noblest Americans who ever lived, and one of the greatest captains known to the annals of war' —who believed that 'secession would do no good' but had placed his loyalty to his native state before his allegiance to the government he served: in Grant who accepted Lee's surrender: in Sherman and in 'Stonewall' Jackson, it threw up on either side a succession of magnificent commanders. But the cost of the first modern war in history was enormous: it took the lives of almost three-quarters of a million men. The Southern states were ruined, and their economic progress was held up for many years to come; while Lincoln fell to a Southern assassin soon after the celebration of victory.

497 After successes in the western campaigns, General ULYSSES S. GRANT (1822-85) was appointed Commander-in-Chief in March 1864 and led the Union forces to victory in Virginia; photographed in front of his tent at Cold Harbor

'Reconstruction' and
the Years of Isolation

Had Lincoln survived, the period of 'Reconstruction' might have been far less painful and ignominious. As it was, although the military terms had been generous, the South received little mercy from the hostile

498 **The Confederate capital in flames; the CITY OF RICHMOND, Virginia, seen from across the James River on May 20, 1865, six weeks after Lee's surrender at Appomattox Courthouse**

politicians of the North; and not until 1877 did a more conciliatory and constructive spirit prevail. Simultaneously, American statesmen developed a not unnatural distrust of Europe. Had not a large proportion of contemporary Englishmen favoured the cause of the Confederate rebels? True, such Radical thinkers as Cobden and Bright, expressing the views of the lower classes, were fervent abolitionists; but the upper and middle classes had proved generally sympathetic to the South, and Gladstone had spoken with warm regard of the Southern leaders and of their attempts to build a new nation.

The history of the United States, between the end of the Civil War and the American declaration of war against Germany in April 1917, may be divided into two main phases. First came a long period of political and national self-absorption, during which the eyes of the American people were customarily focused on their own affairs, and their interests were chiefly concentrated upon the tremendous drama

499　During the Presidency of Theodore Roosevelt, when the United States first emerged as a world power, New Yorkers stroll along snow-banked pavements between the sober brownstone houses of FIFTH AVENUE

of their own domestic growth, as immense territories were opened up, huge natural resources were tapped and exploited, a vast influx of immigrants flowed through their gates and gigantic commercial empires were established by an enterprising few. In this period, modern Americanism came into being, heralded by impressive achievements in industry, engineering and all the practical arts. The finer arts followed more slowly and awaited a new century before American example began to make a revolutionary impact on the thought, taste and manners of Europe, and, eventually, of the world. During the first half of the old century, the United States had symbolized for Europe a noble conception of freedom. As the era drew to a close, it became synonymous to the outsider with the idea of wealth and individual opportunity. Within the country, however, the Populist movement of the 1890s embodied a recurring theme in American politics: the revolt of the smaller man in the West and South against the formidable money-power of the East. Although the Populist candidates never won the Presidency, most of the progressive reforms they urged were accepted in the twentieth century and eventually became law.

Imperialists and Idealists

For American idealism, as it affected issues both national and international, was always apparent not far beneath the surface, despite the inward-looking mood that had developed since the Civil War. As late as 1895, Anglo-American relations passed through an extremely serious crisis, when President Cleveland fired off at the British Prime Minister, Lord Salisbury, what he called 'a twenty-inch gun note' on the subject of a dispute over the boundaries of British Guiana and Venezuela that

500 **On the White House portico before they drove together to the Capitol on March 4, 1913, the retiring President WILLIAM HOWARD TAFT (1857 - 1930) stands with his successor WOODROW WILSON (1856-1924)**

seemed to threaten the sanctity of the time-honoured Monroe Doctrine. Armed conflict appeared to be imminent, before the problem was eventually solved by more cautious diplomatic methods. Thereafter relations slowly improved between the two great English-speaking countries, as the German threat darkened the British sky, and the United States awoke to a recognition of the part that it must play as an international power.

Thus the second period of American development shows among American statesmen a growing sense of international responsibility. Although Theodore Roosevelt on the American continent was an enthusiastic advocate of the 'big stick', and had earned popular renown as the bellicose hero of the Spanish-American War of 1898, abroad he was a keen advocate of the operations of the Hague Tribunal and believed that the welfare of the United States was inextricably bound up with that of Europe. When war exploded in Europe, he attacked President Wilson's neutral stand; and, the United States having entered the War, he sought permission to organize and lead a volunteer contingent. From the European point of view, Woodrow Wilson is American idealism personified: to many of his countrymen, the type of American idealist thrown to the European wolf pack. Wilson's story is tragic and heroic. Certainly he failed in most of his chief objectives: the concert of nations he had envisaged, thanks to the ruthlessness of post-war nationalism, remained an insubstantial dream. But he had committed his country to a course of action from which it could not permanently draw back. Nothing about his existence so became him as the manner in which he tried and failed.

The Civil War

502 **LINCOLN VISITS FIELD HEADQUARTERS,** shortly after the campaign of the Antietam, September 1862, in which Lee's threat to Washington was repulsed in costly battles by General George G. McClellan

501   **The fanatical abolitionist who seized the United States arsenal at Harpers Ferry and planned to set up a free stronghold for fugitive slaves; JOHN BROWN (1800-59) climbing the steps of the scaffold to meet his death at Charles Town**

503 *(below)* **LINCOLN UP A TREE;** a cartoon of January 1862, when British opinion was inflamed by the 'Trent' affair, in which the Federal navy seized two Southern commissioners from a British mail steamer

"UP A TREE."
Colonel Bull and the Yankee 'Coon.
'Coon. "AIR YOU IN ARNEST, COLONEL?"
Colonel Bull. "I AM."
'Coon. "DON'T FIRE—I'LL COME DOWN."

504 One of the battles in the West, where the Union forces steadily made progress; PEA RIDGE, ARKANSAS; the Federal's decisive advance under General Samuel R. Curtis, on March 8, 1862

505 (*below*) Gettysburg put an end to Southern hopes of winning the war by a victory on Northern soil; THREE CONFEDERATE SOLDIERS captured in the battle, dishevelled but defiant

On July 1-3, 1863, at Gettysburg, Pennsylvania, Lee's army was fought to a standstill by General George G. Meade and Southern fortunes entered on their decline. General JAMES LONGSTREET'S attack on the Federal left, July 2, 507. Some of the CONFEDERATE DEAD, 506 *top*

The Civil War continues

508   **CITY POINT**, Virginia, on the James River, one of General Grant's supply-depots in the last stages of the war

509   **Photography recorded the grimness of the war: the END OF A CONFEDERATE SHARP-SHOOTER below Big Round Top at Gettysburg**

510   **An episode in the fiercely contested war at sea; IRON-CLAD CONFEDERATE GUN-BOATS attack the Union blockading squadron off the city of Charleston, South Carolina**

511 The war was fought with every type of modern weapon; a 13-inch MONSTER MORTAR, used during Grant's siege of Petersburg in the summer of 1864

512 Lincoln's first call to arms brought 75,000 men to the colours, and half a million followed in the ensuing months; the battle-stained flag of the 8th PENNSYLVANIA RESERVES

513 (below) The RUINS OF CHARLESTON, where the war had begun on April 12, 1861, after the naval bombardment that led to its capitulation on February 17, 1865

ONE OF MR. ROOSEVELT'S QUIET DAYS

He attends to San Domingo

He hands Mr. Castro a few

He jumps on the Senate

He writes on the race question

He lands on the Standard Oil Co.

He attends a banquet in New York

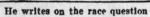

He superintends the preparations for inauguration day

He passes a hot message to the Senate

He pauses a moment to make plans for a hunting trip

516 (*below*) **An apostle of the 'strenuous life', Theodore Roosevelt (1858-1919) commanded a regiment of 'Rough Riders', raised by himself, in the Spanish-American War of 1898. ROOSEVELT AT THE BATTLE OF ST JUAN HILL**

515 **Born campaigner and bellicose reformer, THEODORE ROOSEVELT (1858-1919) at home waged an intrepid, if inconclusive, war against the monopolistic practices of Big Business, attacking the rapid growth of the trusts that conflicted with his idea of individual liberty**

American politics

517 **WOODROW WILSON AND HIS CAMPAIGN REPORTER:** chief architect of the League of Nations; 'His career,' an historian has written, 'like that of Coriolanus, is far nobler in its defeat than the success stories of many lesser men'

American life

518 In 1838 the famous transatlantic vessel the 'Great Western' had crossed the Atlantic in fifteen days. By 1858 screw propellors were superseding paddle-wheels. **SALOON OF A STEAMBOAT** about 1870, on the New York-Boston run

520 In the age of the crinoline, **AMELIA JENKS BLOOMER** (1818-94), a particularly unselfconscious feminist, was the first to advocate rational dress for women. Mrs Bloomer, wearing the odd costume she had devised, on an English song sheet

519 **COTTON BALES**—the foundation of Southern wealth—start on their long journey towards northern markets. At the beginning of the nineteenth century, thanks to the invention of the cotton gin, over seventeen million pounds of American cotton were exported every year

521 In the remoter regions of some Southern States, during the period that followed the Civil War, bitter domestic feuding was not uncommon. A Kentucky patriarch, 'DEVIL ANSE' HATFIELD, with his embattled family

522 The life of the cattle-herder, on the vast unfenced ranches of the West, became an important part of the great American legend. COWBOYS AROUND A WAGGON, in an early photograph

Writers and painters

524   The New World's most magnificent gift to European literature, **HENRY JAMES** (1843-1916) became a British citizen in 1915. His penetrating psychological insight endowed the modern novel with a new dimension

523   **Son of an American army engineer, JAMES ABBOTT MCNEILL WHISTLER** (1834-1903) reached Europe in 1855, and remained to propagate the gospel of art for its own sake, with the help of a delicately sensitive brush and an exceptionally biting wit

525   **Type of the homespun American sage, rich in simple native shrewdness, MARK TWAIN** (1835-1910) revealed his true literary gifts when he evoked the memories of his early youth, and published 'Tom Sawyer' and 'Huckleberry Finn'

526 The earliest version of 'Leaves of Grass' appeared in 1855, when Emerson wrote a congratulatory letter to its unknown author WALT WHITMAN (1819-92), the first American poet to break away from conventional poetic forms

527 From the material furnished by his own adventurous life, HERMAN MELVILLE (1819-91) wove a series of novels that have made a permanent contribution to the art of imaginative fiction. 'Moby-Dick' was published in 1851

The revolution

in transport

528   **During the eighteen-seventies, the tracks of the new ELEVATED RAILWAY began to snake across Manhattan. This photograph, showing the rear of a train and its steam locomotive on the right, was taken in 1884**

529   **In 1829 two locomotives were imported from England by the Delaware and Hudson Canal Company. Only forty years later, a railroad spanned the whole continent. Early picture of a TRAIN CROSSING NIAGARA BRIDGE**

530 **About 1910, the modern automobile emerged in triumph from a period of trial and error, under the masterful direction of such pioneers as Henry Ford. THE END OF A MODEL 'T' ASSEMBLY LINE, 1913**

531 **Re-launched for a modern celebration, an AIRCRAFT OF THE 1910 PUSHER-TYPE sails off on an anniversary flight. In 1903, Orville and Wilbur Wright made their first successful experiments with a power-driven aeroplane**

Plate XX **A village in 1802, already incorporated as a city in 1819, destined to become the second largest city of Ohio, CINCINATTI, here shown as it appeared in 1872, typifies the rapid process of commercial and industrial growth that was taking place throughout the continent**

The growth of industry

532   Three months' schooling at the age of seven prepared **THOMAS ALVA EDISON** (1847-1931) for his career as one of the greatest inventors of the century, to whom we owe the telephone and the first practical incandescent lamp

533   From a farm near Cleveland, Ohio, **JOHN D. ROCKEFELLER** (1839-1937) set out, when he was sixteen years old, to found a gigantic industrial empire, larger, richer and more extensive than the average European kingdom

534   The first steel-framed modern skyscraper sprang from the Chicago skyline in 1883. New York's stark and dramatic **FLATIRON BUILDING** was constructed in the year 1902

XVI

EDWARD VII AND GEORGE V

The human method of dividing time into decades and centuries is, of course, an artificial one. Yet it is a curious fact that, when the century changes, the transition is often accompanied by a far-reaching change in the spiritual and intellectual climate. So it happened at the outset of the twentieth century; and on this occasion the opening of a new age coincided with the beginning of a new reign. The long Victorian epoch now gave way to a brief Edwardian interlude; and Edward VII, whom his masterful mother had deliberately excluded from the active conduct of affairs, proved to be a sovereign of a very different, and much less conservative, type. Edwardian society, over which he presided, bore very little resemblance to the Victorian social order. A tremendous gulf still yawned between the world of privilege and the world of poverty; but many of the King's own friends appeared to have been chosen for their wealth and ability

535 **A ROYAL SHOOTING PARTY AT WINDSOR,** November 1907. In the front row, King Edward VII (1901-10), with the Empress of Germany and the future Queen Mary on his right: the moustachioed Emperor and Queen Alexandra appear immediately behind him

to amuse him rather than for their social distinction or their intellectual gifts; and the English upper classes followed suit by welcoming, and intermarrying with, a host of social newcomers. While English grandees bestowed their hands and titles upon transatlantic heiresses, South African millionaires, fresh from the diamond fields, entertained lavishly in Park Lane.

It was a period of peace, prosperity and ostentation; and in the role of diplomatic peacemaker the King himself showed unexpected skill. Thus his personal influence contributed to the establishment of the *Entente Cordiale* with France; and the public at large, who had often admired his worldliness, also came to value the reputation that he now earned for international shrewdness. It was felt that, so long as he ruled, Great Britain would steer clear of any European conflict:

> 'There'll be no war
> As long as we've a king like good King Edward;
> 'E never did 'old with that sort of thing.'

sang a popular comedian of the age.

Beneath the surface, however, behind the splendid pageant of the London 'seasons', forces were already at work that would soon transform the social landscape. Labour was demanding its due, although at the opening of the century only two Labour members sat in the House

536 In Great Britain, the establishment of the ENTENTE CORDIALE with France was hailed as a triumph of the King's diplomatic skill. EDWARD VII AND PRESIDENT FALLIERES at the Franco-British Exhibition of May 1908

of Commons; and the English Radical movement, largely dormant since 1848, began to raise its head again. Simultaneously, Liberalism re-arose; and at the General Election of 1906 the Liberals came back with a triumphant majority. A Liberal government continued to rule the country from 1905 to 1915. In 1910, it twice challenged, and twice defeated, the obstructive House of Lords.

The struggle of the classes had its counterpart in a resounding battle of the sexes. The Emancipated Woman had first made her appearance during the latter half of the man-dominated nineteenth century. Now the 'New Woman' returned as the Suffragette; and militant crusaders for woman's right to vote shook the sang-froid of the British people. The House of Commons itself was invaded; and, at a race-meeting in the reign of George V, a suffragette, who had climbed the rails, met her death under the hooves of the King's horse. Asquith's government decided to stand firm; and there were bitter feminist complaints against the savage injustice of official measures.

The Approach to War

Meanwhile Ireland—an age-old source of anxiety—became year by year a heavier problem; and the British government's attempt to solve it by offering Irish nationalists Home Rule aroused the wrath of 'Loyal Ulster'. Northern Ireland threatened to fight rather than to

537 **With the war-cry VOTES FOR WOMEN! Sylvia Pankhurst and her fellow sufragettes launched a fierce campaign against the Asquith government. Here, in the arms of an embarrassed police inspector, she is being removed from the railings of Buckingham Palace, May 21, 1914**

538 **GEORGE BERNARD SHAW** (1856-1950); the unsuccessful novelist, turned critic and playwright, brought an Irish wit and an Irish love of paradox to the castigation of the Anglo-Saxon world; student of Marx and a founding father of the Socialist Fabian Society

accept incorporation with the South; for a while, the so-called United Kingdom seemed to be drifting towards civil strife. This threat was averted not by diplomacy at home but by the explosion abroad of a far more serious conflict. The heir to the Austro-Hungarian throne was assassinated at Sarajevo; Germany rallied to the support of Austria; Russia and France, presently joined by England, ranged themselves upon the opposite side. By August 4, 1914, when Great Britain declared war on Germany, the embattled nations of Europe were making ready for the final test.

The England over which Edward VII had ruled from 1901 to 1910, and his son George V was dutifully ruling on the outbreak of the First World War, disappeared in the summer of 1914, never again to re-emerge. But during those thirteen years its record of progress was by no means inconsiderable. Important social reforms had been set on foot—some of them under the direction of that enterprising young Minister Mr Winston Churchill; the barriers of caste and privilege were being slowly broken down—David Lloyd George's provisions for social betterment in his Budget of 1909 heralded the modern Welfare State; and English literature, particularly the English novel, entered on a new and adventurous phase. H. G. Wells, Arnold Bennett, Joseph Conrad, George Moore, John Galsworthy, Bernard Shaw, all prospered in the new era; and Wells's novels, and Shaw's and Galsworthy's plays, were usually inspired by a passionate concern with some important social issue. It was a bad world, they implied, but a world capable of rapid and decisive improvement. They could not foresee how many illusions would vanish beneath the deluge of a European war.

539   Like most wars in British history, the First World War began with a sharp reverse for British arms. During the RETREAT FROM MONS, in the late summer of 1914, British cavalrymen ride through a French village. Soon cavalry engagements were to be superseded by trench warfare

540   DAVID LLOYD GEORGE (1863-1945); in his youth a fiery Radical and eloquent critic of British imperial policy, he became after 1916 a puissant Allied war-leader. Seen with the Conservative chief, Andrew Bonar Law (1858-1923)

Men of power

542   Prime Minister for eight years from 1908, HERBERT HENRY ASQUITH (1852-1928), a man of varied intellectual interests, surmounted the decisive conflict with the House of Lords, struggled with the Irish problem and presided over the opening years of the First World War

541   Appointed Prime Minister in December 1905, SIR HENRY CAMPBELL-BANNERMAN (1836-1908) led the Liberal party to electoral victory and launched his Government upon a broadly reforming programme

543   Founder of modern British journalism, ALFRED HARMSWORTH, VISCOUNT NORTHCLIFFE (1865-1922), used the lively power of his newspapers to wage a succession of vigorous political campaigns

544   Consolidator of the Entente with France and Russia, SIR EDWARD GREY (1862-1933), Foreign Secretary, 1905-16, was a member of an aristocratic Liberal family that had played a shaping role in nineteenth-century history

545   Aristocrat and philosopher-statesman, ARTHUR JAMES BALFOUR (1848-1930) was Conservative Prime Minister from 1902 until 1905 and served as Foreign Secretary in Lloyd George's war-time coalition

546   Caricatured by the delicate pencil of Sir Max Beerbohm (1872-1956), SIR EDWARD CARSON (1854-1935), the champion of Ulster and opponent of Irish Home Rule, is here depicted in sabre-rattling mood

Changing society

547 **ASCOT FASHIONS**, 1910, during the period of mourning for King Edward. From wasp waists descend voluminous skirts closely moulded to the wearer's hips; while huge circular feathered hats, secured by veils and numerous pins, perch insecurely upon the summit of the head

548 The Edwardian age saw the rise of the Labour movement. **JAMES KEIR HARDY** (1856-1915), a Scottish miner, was the first leader of the Parliamentary Labour party. Here, in leonine pose amid the lions of Trafalgar Square, he addresses a suffragette meeting

549 One of the American beauties to bestow their hands on English noblemen was Miss Margaretta Drexel of Philadelphia, who became **COUNTESS OF WINCHILSEA** in 1910. Drawing by John Singer Sargent (1856-1925)

550 The summer of 1914 was particularly warm and sunny. A riverside assembly at **HENLEY REGATTA**. The young woman reclining on the right of the photograph adventurously smokes a cigarette, a habit that was beginning to grow even among the middle classes

Writers and the stage

551 The famous series of 'Wessex novels', inspired by the scenes and characters of his rustic youth, came to an abrupt end in 1896; and thereafter THOMAS HARDY (1840-1928) devoted his gifts to the drama and to the composition of curiously original poems

552 A star of light opera, MISS GABRIELLE RAY: she looked, Cecil Beaton writes, as if butter would not have melted in her mouth; 'but there was an intriguing perversity about such excessive prettiness'

553 In 1912, MRS PATRICK CAMPBELL (1865-1940) created the part of Shaw's Eliza Doolittle; and for many years her beauty and wit continued to delight the dramatist. Here she is seen with the celebrated actor-manager George Alexander

554 **Provincial adventurer with cosmopolitan leanings, ARNOLD BENNETT (1867-1931) applied to the English novel some of the literary lessons he had from French masters. 'The Old Wives' Tale', his greatest achievement, was published in the year 1908**

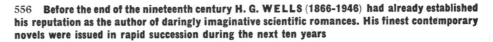

556 **Before the end of the nineteenth century H. G. WELLS (1866-1946) had already established his reputation as the author of daringly imaginative scientific romances. His finest contemporary novels were issued in rapid succession during the next ten years**

555 **Across the Irish Sea in Dublin, a new literary movement, coloured by Celtic nationalist sentiment, had begun to develop during the eighteen-nineties. Among its most romantic leaders was the visionary poet W. B. YEATS (1865-1939); portrait by Augustus John**

First World War

557 **AUGUST 1914, in London; a recruiting car, marked 'On His Majesty's Service', drives down the Strand, past a poster of war news; military conscription was introduced only in 1916**

558 The victor of Omdurman and subduer of the South African Boers, Field-Marshal **EARL KITCHENER** (1850-1916), as Secretary of State for War carried out a vast expansion of the British army; he inspects the Honourable Artillery Company, 1915

560 Commander of the battlecruiser fleet in the actions of Heligoland Bight, Dogger Bank and Jutland, the dashing Admiral EARL BEATTY (1871-1936), later First Sea Lord

559 Commonwealth troops fought successfully on many Allied fronts; KING GEORGE V (1910-36) INSPECTING THE 2ND AUSTRALIAN DIVISION with General Sir Henry Rawlinson (*left*)

562 The British Commander-in-Chief in France, Field-Marshal EARL HAIG (1861-1928); despite the antagonism between the Prime Minister and himself, his painstaking generalship culminated in victory

561 Commander of the Grand Fleet which he led in the controversial Battle of Jutland, 1916, Admiral EARL JELLICOE (1859-1935) on board his flagship, H.M.S. IRON DUKE

XVII

FROM
WORLD WAR
TO WORLD WAR

America's intervention in the First World War came at a critical time for Great Britain and her Allies. In April 1917 over three-quarters of a million tons of Allied shipping had been sunk, the morale of the Allied troops in France was at a low ebb, and Russia, stricken by revolution, was virtually out of the war. The entry of America gave the Allies new hope; it brought them financial security, and it enabled Britain to press the blockade of the German ports. In the spring of 1918 the effectiveness of this blockade induced the Germans to undertake a series of massive military offensives on the Western front, and the Allies were driven back many miles behind their lines. By summer, as the millionth American soldier arrived in Europe, heavy counteroffensives were launched and the tide turned. Within a few months Germany was forced to sue for peace.

America had entered to war to protect the rights of neutrals, but her aims had quickly broadened to embrace the cause of ultimate world peace. Her hopes of establishing it on a firm foundation, however, were to be sadly disappointed. The chief object of President Woodrow Wilson, an idealist who passionately believed in America's civilizing mission, was to set up an international system—a League of Nations—to ensure the end of war. But when the Peace Treaty, together with the Covenant of the League incorporated in it, was presented to the Senate for ratification, it failed—though by a very narrow margin—to gain the required two-thirds majority. Thus it happened that the League of Nations, the one hopeful product of the war, started life with what proved to be an insuperable handicap, the abstention of America.

563 **The leader, and virtually the creator, of the American Expeditionary Force in the First World War, GENERAL PERSHING** (1860-1948) **arrives for an investiture at Hyde Park, London, in July 1919, accompanied by the Prince of Wales, Winston Churchill (then Secretary of State for War) and the American Ambassador, J. W. Davis**

Plate XXI (*opposite*) **The great dome of the CAPITOL AT WASHINGTON soon came to symbolize for the whole world the classic foundations on which American democracy rests, and the strength and dignity of purpose that have inspired its growth**

564 **At the Versailles Conference in 1919, THE 'BIG FOUR'**, Lloyd George of Britain, Orlando of Italy, Clemenceau of France and President Wilson of the United States, attempted to create a new world out of the ruins of the old

565 **Son of a Scottish labourer, RAMSAY MACDONALD** (1866-1937) became Prime Minister of the first Labour Government in 1924, and again in 1929. On the formation of the National Government in 1931, he remained Prime Minister when most of his Socialist colleagues resigned

Conforming to the mood of the people, the new President, Warren G. Harding, an undistinguished Republican Senator from Ohio, preached a return to what he called 'normalcy'. 'We seek no part,' he said on taking office, 'in directing the affairs of the world.'

America in the twenties was the scene of unprecedented industrial boom. For Britain, on the other hand, it was a period of recurring slump, with unemployment figures, particularly in the mining areas, running dangerously high. In 1924 a Labour Prime Minister, Ramsay MacDonald, gained office, and two years later the whole labour movement came out in support of a General Strike, one of the critical events in English social history. The strike was overcome by a Conservative Government, but at the next Election, in 1929, Labour for the first time gained a majority over any other single party.

In America the industrial boom went hand in hand with a meteoric increase in speculation. It was widely believed that every American would soon enrich himself with common stocks and that a new era had dawned. But the new era was that of the Crash. In one day, late in October 1929, some thirty billion dollars of paper money vanished into nothing. Over twelve million people were put out of work. A whole generation was permanently scarred. President Hoover, who had taken over from Coolidge only six months before, struggled unsuccessfully with the crisis, and in the election of 1932 he was swept out of office by Franklin D. Roosevelt, the Democratic candidate. Roosevelt promised a New Deal, and instituted a series of far-reaching social and economic reforms. A huge public works programme was launched, with the double aim of creating jobs and developing the resources of the country. While these measures brought much relief, full prosperity did not return until defence spending got under way in 1940–1.

In Britain, the depression brought a new wave of unemployment and the prospect of national bankruptcy. Ramsay MacDonald resigned in 1931, declaring that his party could not face the crisis alone, and the subsequent Coalition Government, first under MacDonald, and then under the Conservative leader Stanley Baldwin, radically changed Britain's monetary and commercial policies. She abandoned both the gold standard and Free Trade. The thirties became for Britain a period of gradually returning prosperity.

The British Monarchy and Commonwealth

The thirties also brought a new relationship between Britain and her overseas Empire. By the Statute of Westminster, the British Parliament formally renounced all legislative power over the Dominions—Canada, Australia, New Zealand and South Africa—which nevertheless remained united to Britain by common allegiance to the Crown. This development brought a new importance to the British monarchy, which in 1936 received a serious challenge. George V, after a reign of twenty-six years, was succeeded by his eldest son. Edward VIII, who had achieved great popularity as Prince of Wales, was universally acclaimed. But when it became known that he wished to marry an American lady who had been twice divorced, a wave of controversy rocked the country. Parliament stood firmly behind Baldwin in opposition to the marriage, and Edward abdicated

The menace of Hitler

In the wake of inflation, despair and mass unemployment, the Nazi party rose to power in Germany, and Hitler, in open defiance of the League, began intensive rearmament. In 1936 he reoccupied the Rhineland, and two years later annexed Austria and encircled Czecho-slovakia. Neville Chamberlain, who had succeeded Baldwin, met Hitler and Mussolini in Munich, and returned to herald 'peace in our time'. The peace was short-lived. In March 1939 Hitler marched into Prague and in September he turned on Poland. Chamberlain's optimism was proved mistaken, and war was declared on Germany by Britain and France. In the following year, amid the clash of defeat, Chamberlain's government fell from power. It was replaced by a national coalition under Winston Churchill, who became a prime architect of eventual victory.

During the thirties the Americans were too deeply involved in their own domestic problems to give much thought to Europe. Many of those who were inclined to sympathize with Britain were disillusioned by what they considered to be her 'abandonment' of Abyssinia, Spain and Czechoslovakia to the dictators. American isolationist sentiment was particularly strong in the Midwest. The opinion spread that America had been unwise after all to intervene in the First World War. Between 1935 and 1937, three Neutrality Acts were passed through Congress. At the outbreak of war, most Americans had been hostile to Hitler; but it was generally supposed that Britain and France would be able to halt him. The fall of France came as a sudden shock. As the Battle of Britain proceeded under Churchill's leadership, there was growing sympathy and alarm. At the Presidential Election of 1940, both Roosevelt and his Republican opponent, Wendell Wilkie, declared themselves for 'all aid short of war'. Roosevelt was returned—the first American President to obtain a third term.

Early in 1941 he obtained the passage of the Lend-Lease Act through Congress, whereby Britain was allowed indispensable war supplies

566 **At the Munich Conference of 1938, the sincere, deeply peace-loving, ever-trustful attitude of NEVILLE CHAMBERLAIN** (1869-1940) con-trasts with the arrogant self-confidence of Hitler and **MUSSOLINI**

without payment. Now, in spite of her concern for neutrality, America geared herself to the cause of Britain. But the United States were finally brought into the conflict not by Germany but by Japan. The Japanese had long since been prosecuting their imperialist designs: in 1931 they had invaded Manchuria—the first open breach of the League's Covenant—and in 1937 had started a war with China. On the morning of Sunday, December 7, 1941, Japan made an attack on the Pearl Harbour naval base at Hawaii. Four days later Germany and Italy declared war on the United States.

567 Among the major advantages enjoyed by the Allies in the second World War was the close friendship that grew up between PRESIDENT ROOSEVELT and WINSTON CHURCHILL, seen here at Washington in December 1941, only two weeks after the entry of the United States into the war

568 **WOODROW WILSON** (1856-1924) inspired the League of Nations but failed to win Congressional approval for America's membership of the new world organization

569 **CALVIN COOLIDGE** (1872-1933) assumed office on the death of President Harding, and was elected for a full term in 1924. Born on a Vermont farm, he was Governor of Massachusetts 1917-20

Kings and Presidents

570 The popularity of **KING GEORGE V AND QUEEN MARY** reached its apex at their Silver Jubilee in 1935. 'I had no idea that the people felt like that about me,' the King said. 'They must like me for myself.' Despite his high regard for the idea of Kingship, he was an essentially modest man.

571　During his brief reign, EDWARD VIII took a great personal interest in the problem of British unemployment. Here he is seen touring a distressed industrial area of South Wales in November 1936, only a few weeks before his abdication

572　(*left*) PRESIDENT FRANKLIN D. ROOSEVELT (1882-1945), like Churchill in Britain, had his critics in his own country, but was almost universally admired overseas. Having led the United States out economic depression, he led them to victory in the Second World War

573　A Prime Minister who will live among the very greatest names in British history was a devoted servant of the Crown. GEORGE VI AND HIS QUEEN visit Winston Churchill at 10 Downing Street in the early years of the Second World War

People and politics

574   **LADY ASTOR, American-born, was the first woman to take her seat in the House of Commons. She is seen campaigning in her constituency at Plymouth during the early 1920s**

293

577 (below) **THE GREAT DEPRESSION** of the early 30s created temporary chaos in the lives of millions of Americans. To alleviate the distress, allotments were made over by municipalities (here at **Long Beach, California**) to provide the unemployed with a wage and the destitute with food

575 The **BRITISH GENERAL STRIKE** in 1926 led to more threats of violence than actual incidents, and ended in the political defeat of the strikers. A petrol wagon is escorted by mounted police in London

576 **STANLEY BALDWIN** (1867-1947) was Prime Minister three times between the wars. An industrialist by upbringing, he was shrewd, simple and sincere. 'My mind moves slowly', was a typically disarming admission by one of the astutest men in politics

578 (right) **Out of the depression emerged the New Deal. Its most publicized achievement was the Tennessee Valley Authority which constructed huge engineering works, like the KENTUCKY DAM, for hydro-electric power and flood-control**

Arts and entertainment

579   **BROADCASTING**, comparable in cultural influence to the invention of printing, had its British beginning in 1922, and by 1926, when this play was broadcast, the BBC was an established national institution

580   **VIRGINIA WOOLF** (1882-1941), author of 'Orlando', 'Mrs Dalloway' and many other books, was one of the most gifted novelists and critics of her time, and had a profound influence on English intellectual life

581 **The English recall with pride that CHARLIE CHAPLIN was born a Londoner.** Seen here in 1920 with officers of the U.S. Marine Corps and Jackie Coogan, he was already the most loved comedian of both countries

582 **Baseball has produced its national heroes in the United States, as cricket has in England. BABE RUTH** (1895-1948) was the most idolized of them all.

THE PRESENT DAY

583 **WESTMINSTER ABBEY** did not escape the German air-attacks on London, but the damage to this most venerable of English churches was fortunately not great. Ten years later it was the scene of the magnificent ceremony opposite

The bombing of Pearl Harbour, the greatest disaster ever inflicted on the army and navy of the United States, made a tremendous emotional impact on the American people. During the First World War there had been a feeling in America that her troops 'were pulling someone else's chestnuts out of the fire', that the peace of the world was being settled for European interests. Now America was suddenly forced into a global conflict on her own account. She entered the war not as an 'associated power', as she had in 1917, but as a fully fledged partner in a Grand Alliance. The Second World War was to be the greatest Anglo-American enterprise in the history of the two countries.

Shortly after the attack on Pearl Harbour, Japan overran the Far East. During the next three-and-a-half years, a series of desperate campaigns in the Pacific was terminated by the dropping of two atomic bombs on Japan, although the Japanese Government had begun to make overtures for peace through Russia and was already a half-defeated nation. Meanwhile in the Mediterranean, the British Army's victories in North Africa led to the Anglo-American invasion of Sicily and Italy. In January 1944, General Eisenhower became Supreme Commander of the Allied Expeditionary Force that landed in Normandy for the final stage of the offensive in Europe. Germany capitulated on May 8, 1945, and the capitulation of Japan followed three months later.

After the

Second World War

In the first two or three years after the war, most Americans settled back easily into normal life. The depression had been scotched and industry geared itself to a new era of prosperity. There were signs of a

Plate XXII (*opposite*) **The Coronation in 1953 of QUEEN ELIZABETH II,** here surrounded by bishops and the highest noblemen in the country, deepened the respect and affection with which the young Queen was held on both sides of the Atlantic

post-war mood similar to the mood after the First World War: a thirst for education and travel by demobilized G.I.s; an increase in crime statistics (this time for juvenile delinquency); changes in fashion (this time a New Look from Dior that made skirts longer); everywhere a passion for new gadgets. Politically, there was a swing to the right: the Republicans gained control of both Houses of Congress in the mid-term elections of 1946, and the Taft-Hartley Act of the following year introduced severe restraints on organized labour. Nevertheless, a Democrat remained in the White House—President Truman, who, as Vice-President, had succeeded Roosevelt on his death early in 1945. Truman survived the subsequent election in 1948, but in 1952 a Republican, Eisenhower, was returned for the first time in twenty years. Eisenhower achieved a second term in 1956.

In Britain, on the other hand, as in 1918, the picture was much gloomier. The economy was in a perilous state. At the General Election of 1945 Churchill's Conservative Party was defeated and Clement Attlee came to power at the head of a Labour Government. Many Americans saw in the election result ingratitude on the part of the British towards their war-leader: in fact, it was due to a reaction against pre-war Conservative Government, which Churchill himself had often criticized, and to the electorate's desire for a New Deal. With national-ization in the forefront of its programme, the new Labour Government brought many basic industries—coal, gas, electricity, road and rail transport—under public ownership. An extensive social security pro-gramme was introduced, including a National Health scheme launched by Aneurin Bevan as Minister of Health. Labour, after winning the 1950 election by a narrow margin, was defeated in the following year, when Churchill became Prime Minister again, and at the two subse-quent elections, in 1955 and 1959. In the latter election, Hugh Gaitskell led the Labour Party, and Harold Macmillan the Conserva-tives. In spite of their three successive set-backs, Labour, during their period of office after the war, had helped to advance a social revolution in Britain, the effects of which—a general levelling of incomes through taxation and a breaking down of much of the old class system—were to remain.

America and Britain

The post-war years also saw the withdrawal of Britain from many of her traditional overseas possessions. In 1947 India was divided into two sovereign states, India and Pakistan, and in the following year Ceylon

584   Two new leaders of America and Britain took the places of Roosevelt and Churchill at the end of the war with Germany. PRESIDENT HARRY S. TRUMAN and CLEMENT ATTLEE, the latter accompanied by his Foreign Secretary, Ernest Bevin, meet at the Potsdam Conference

585 (below) In 1954 WINSTON CHURCHILL was again Prime Minister, and ANTHONY EDEN his Foreign Secretary. They are seen with PRESIDENT EISENHOWER and JOHN FOSTER DULLES, Secretary of State, at the White House in June of that year

586   The United States led the free nations of the
world in the fight against Communist aggression
in KOREA, assisted by the forces of her international allies. A group of Koreans are assembled
under the United Nations flag

received Dominion status. Throughout the globe, Britain was faced by
a growing tide of nationalism. Her answer to this situation was to
evolve a new relationship with many of her former possessions within
an enlarged Commonwealth. The events of the post-war world soon
emphasized the fundamental community of interest between America
and Britain. Long before the war ended, it seemed clear that the United
States would not tread—or be able to tread—the same isolationist path
as she had trodden in the twenties and thirties. She played a leading
part in the United Nations, and became the proponent of a new force
in the world—American liberalism—compounded partly of idealism,

showing itself in a concern for rehabilitation and relief, and partly of self-interest, that included a desire to create conditions favourable to American economic expansion.

American liberalism soon came into conflict with Russian Communism. The cold war began in earnest in 1948, the year of the Marshall Plan, which envisaged an expenditure of seventeen billion dollars over four years for the recovery of Europe, and of the Truman doctrine, which allotted four hundred million dollars to Greece and Turkey to stiffen them in their resistance to Communism. These measures were denounced by Russia as 'imperialist war-mongering'. In 1949 Britain co-operated with America in relieving the Russian blockade of Berlin, and in the following year both countries were in full agreement over the United States' intervention in Korea. In 1949 NATO was established, the bulwark of collective security in Europe.

The cold war period provided some differences of opinion within Anglo-American co-operation. American policy, backed by the belief that she was superior to the USSR in nuclear weapons, was based on the theory of 'negotiation from strength' and the threat of 'massive retaliation'. Britain was inclined to be cautious, and on a number of occasions—in Korea, for example, and Indo-China—made efforts to restrain the United States from taking an irrevocable step. Britain's attitude to the recognition of Communist China, in particular, led to considerable anti-British feeling in America, which was exploited by, among others, Senator McCarthy. McCarthy's primitive nationalism and witch-hunting were, in turn, regarded with considerable distaste in Britain.

The severest strain on Anglo-American relations came with the Suez crisis of 1956, when Britain intervened in Egypt without American support. Her action produced a sharp division of opinion within the country and was condemned by the United Nations under American leadership.

By the end of 1957 Anglo-American relations had returned to normal. Harold Macmillan, who became Prime Minister on Sir Anthony Eden's resignation at the beginning of 1957, did much to heal the breach, and this growing goodwill was cemented by the immensely popular visits of the Queen and the Duke of Edinburgh to the United States, and of President Eisenhower to Britain. At the opening of the 1960s the two nations found themselves again speaking with a common voice, as well as in a common tongue, for the free world that they had jointly done so much to create and defend.

587　**The biggest figure to emerge in Russia since Stalin's death was NIKITA KHRUSHCHEV, who toured almost every part of the world in an attempt to allay suspicion of Soviet intentions. Here he is greeted in Washington by President Eisenhower in September 1959**

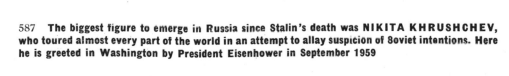

Friends disagree . .

588 The spread of television helped to gain SENATOR McCARTHY the attention of a huge public when he campaigned against the dangers of Communism with a violence that shocked many good citizens in America and Britain

589 *(below)* The Suez crisis of 1956 put a heavy, though temporary, strain on Anglo-American confidence. British troops halted their advance down the line of the SUEZ CANAL in response to the pressure of world opinion, and awaited their replacement by a United Nations' force

590 The British people feared that American support for Chiang Kai-Shek might lead to war with Communist China. An American officer over-looks the off-shore ISLAND OF QUEMOY

.. and Allies co-operate

303

591 Both during and after the war, the two peoples grew to know each other better through the constant presence in Britain of American servicemen. ENGLISH 'BOB-BIES' AND AMERICAN MILITARY POLICE on watch at the corner of a London street

592 (*below*) In 1949 the western Allies were unanimous in resisting the Russian threat to Berlin, and when all other routes to the city were cut, organized the BERLIN AIR-LIFT. The millionth sack of coal is delivered to the beleaguered population

593 The 1955 SUMMIT CONFERENCE AT GENEVA brought together the most powerful men in the world: for the United States, Eisenhower and Dulles; for Britain, Eden and Macmillan; for Russia, Bulganin and Khrushchev. De Gaulle had not yet come to power again in France

594 A traditional source of Anglo-American misunderstanding was the British attitude towards her colonial peoples. HAROLD MACMILLAN IN HIS AFRICAN TOUR of 1960 did much to dispel any remaining suspicion that Britain intended to deny them their democratic rights

A new dimension

596 The United States and Russia competed with each other in the development of rockets, first used in war against a civilian population by Germany. Technicians at Cape Canaveral prepare a **THOR-ABLE ROCKET** for launching

597 Some of the rockets were designed as military missiles; others carried delicate instruments round the world or far into outer space. The 'paddle-wheels' of this **AMERICAN SPACE-CAPSULE** convert sunlight into power for recharging its batteries

595 (*opposite*) The nuclear bomb, the chief deterrent to a fresh outbreak of war, was first developed in the United States, which became incomparably the greatest military power in the Western Alliance

598 Flights by human beings to the moon and beyond were already seriously envisaged in 1960. Here the spacemen are actors on a film set, but the reality was not far distant

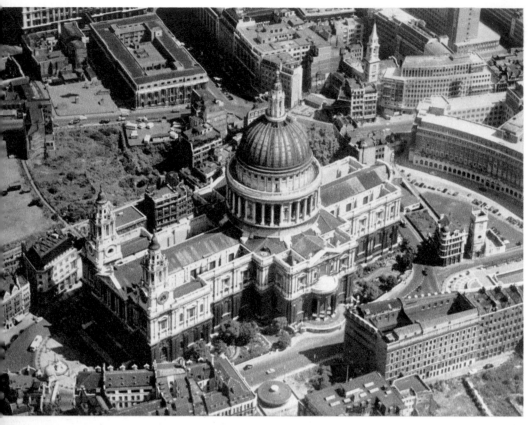

599   St Paul's Cathedral survived the war, but many of the surrounding buildings were totally destroyed. New office blocks in the **CITY OF LONDON** rise from the ruins as evidence of Britain's post-war recovery; the ancient capital wears a fresh face

600   In smaller towns like **PLYMOUTH**, from which Drake had sailed against the Armada and the Pilgrim Fathers set out, new tastes in shopping habits influenced post-war architecture

New

towns

in old

towns

Plate XXIII **New York has long been regarded in Britain as the world-centre of architectural experiment. The GUGGENHEIM MUSEUM of modern art, completed in 1959, was the work of the most famous of modern American architects, Frank Lloyd Wright (1869-1959)**

BRISTOL BASIN

Beneath this east river drive of the city of new york lie stones, bricks and rubble from the bombed city of bristol in england... brought here in ballast from overseas, these fragments that once were homes shall testify while men love freedom to the resolution and fortitude of the people of britain. they saw their homes struck down without warning.... it was not their walls but their valor that kept them free . . . .

———

And broad-based under all
Is planted England's oaken-hearted mood,
As rich in fortitude
As e'er went worldward from the island-wall.

———

ERECTED BY THE
ENGLISH-SPEAKING UNION OF THE UNITED STATES
·· 1942 ··